本書の構成と利用法

それぞれのパートは見開き 2 ページで構成されています。

見開きの左ページ

A 新出単語を主な対象として，単語の意味もしくは英語を書かせる問題です。
A1〜B2は，CEFR-Jでのレベルを表します。A1（易）〜B2（難）です。

B 新出単語を主な対象とした発音問題もしくはアクセント問題です。

C 重要な表現や文法に関する空所補充問題です。

D 重要な表現や文法に関する語句整序問題です。

見開きの右ページ

E 教科書本文の理解を確認する問題です。適語選択や語形変化，語句整序，英問英答など，多様な形式の問題を用意しました。

※本文中のグレーの網かけは，教科書では印字されておらず，音声としてのみ配信している部分であることを示します。

『CEFR-J Wordlist Version 1.6』東京外国語大学投野由紀夫研究室．（URL: http://cefr-j.org/download.htmlより2021年2月ダウンロード）

#Share Your World

Part 1

/50

A Translate the English into Japanese and the Japanese into English.【語彙の知識】（各 1 点）

1. fantastic 形 A2　　　[　　　　　　]　2. enter 動 A2　　　[　　　　　　　]

3. .... 名 B1　コメント　　4. .... 名 A1　楽しみ

5. congratulation 名　　[　　　　　]　6. blossom 名 B2　　　[　　　　　　]

B Choose the word which has primary stress on a different syllable from the other three.【アクセントの知識】　　　　　　　　　　　　　　　　　（各 2 点）

1. ア. cher-ry　　　イ. Eng-lish　　　ウ. en-ter　　　エ. to-day

2. ア. a-gain　　　イ. blos-som　　　ウ. en-trance　　エ. pho-to

3. ア. beau-ti-ful　イ. ex-cit-ing　　ウ. fan-tas-tic　エ. to-geth-er

C Complete the following English sentences to match the Japanese.【表現と文法の知識】

（各 3 点）

1. 母はスマートフォンで初めてメッセージを送った。

My mother sent a message on her smartphone (　　　　　) (　　　　　　)

(　　　　　) (　　　　　　).

2. 私と妹は先週同じシャツを買った。

My sister and I (　　　　　　) the same shirt last week.

3. 今日学校は楽しかったですか。

Did you (　　　　　　) (　　　　　　) at school today?

D Arrange the words in the proper order to match the Japanese.【表現と文法の知識・技能】

（各 3 点）

1. この学校の生徒はとても元気だ。

(are / at / the students / this school) full of energy.

2. 彼が試験に合格して両親はうれしかった。

His parents (glad / he / that / were) passed the exam.

3. トムは家に帰ってテレビでニュースを見た。

Tom (and / home / the news / watched / went) on TV.

E Read the following passage and answer the questions below.

(POSTED by) Manabu

Today was a fantastic day. We (1) our entrance ceremony. Now, I'm a student at Daiichi High School. I studied very hard and (2) this school. I'm glad that Takashi and I (3) to the same school again.

3 Comments

Takashi: I'm glad, (4). Today was a great day. Let's have fun together!

Manabu@Takashi: Yeah! I'm happy (5)(are / here / me / that / with / you).

Vivian: Congratulations! Have an exciting school life!

Manabu@Vivian: Thanks! See you.

David: Congrats! The cherry blossoms in your photo (6) very beautiful.

Manabu@David: Thank you.

1. 空所(1)～(3)に入る最も適当な語を語群から選び，必要なら適切な形に変えなさい。

【語彙と文法の知識】（各2点）

[be, enter, go, have]

(1) (　　　　　　　)　　　(2) (　　　　　　　)　　　(3) (　　　　　　　)

2. 空所(4)に入る最も適当な語を選びなさい。【語彙の知識】 (2点)

ア. also　　　　　イ. and　　　　　ウ. so　　　　　エ. too

3. 下線部(5)の(　　)内の語を適切に並べかえなさい。【表現と文法の知識】 (2点)

4. 空所(6)に入る最も適当な語を選びなさい。【文法の知識】 (2点)

ア. are　　　　　イ. be　　　　　ウ. is　　　　　エ. was

5. 次の問いに英語で答えなさい。【内容についての思考力・判断力・表現力】 (各4点)

(1) What did Manabu do to enter Daiichi High School?

(2) Who wrote comments on Manabu's post?

A Translate the English into Japanese and the Japanese into English.【語彙の知識】（各 1 点）

1. .... 名 B2　広告媒体　　　2. useful 形 A2　　[　　　　　　　]

3. .... 名 B1　プライバシー　　4. .... 形 A2　私的な，個人的な

5. .... 名 A1　問題　　　　　　6. addict 名 B2　　[　　　　　　　]

B Choose the word whose underlined part is pronounced differently from the other three.【発音の知識】　　　　　　　　　　　　　　　　　　　　　　（各 2 点）

1. ア．r<u>u</u>le　　　　イ．sch<u>oo</u>l　　　ウ．st<u>u</u>dy　　　エ．t<u>oo</u>l

2. ア．ad<u>d</u>ict　　　イ．<u>f</u>ind　　　　ウ．li<u>f</u>e　　　　エ．<u>p</u>rivate

3. ア．homew<u>or</u>k　イ．p<u>er</u>sonal　　ウ．sm<u>ar</u>tphone　エ．w<u>or</u>ld

C Complete the following English sentences to match the Japanese.【表現と文法の知識】

（各 3 点）

1. 雨が降っているので今日は家にいるつもりです。

   I (　　　　　　) (　　　　　　　　) home today because it is raining.

2. 具合がよくありません。実際，少し熱があります。

   I don't feel well. (　　　　　　) (　　　　　　　　), I have a little fever.

3. 子供たちが話しかけてくるときは注意を向けてあげよう。

   Let's (　　　　　　) (　　　　　　　) (　　　　　　　　) our kids when they

   talk to us.

D Arrange the words in the proper order to match the Japanese.【表現と文法の知識・技能】

（各 3 点）

1. 私たちは次の 3 月に東京に引っ越す予定です。

   We (are / going / move / to / to) Tokyo next March.

   ....

2. 空に雲はありません。今夜は雨は降らないでしょう。

   There are no clouds in the sky. (it / not / rain / will) tonight.

   ....

3. その教訓を覚えておいてください。

   Please (in / keep / mind / the lesson).

   ....

E Read the following passage and answer the questions below.

Social media are an important part of our daily (1)(life) today. In fact, (2)these useful tools make our lives very exciting. (3), keep some rules in mind when you use social media.

First, pay attention to personal privacy. Don't post private information about you and your friends. If a bad person finds the information, (4)(and your friends / have / some / will / you) problems.

Second, (5) social media for many hours every day. You will easily become a social media addict. Sometimes put down your smartphone and look at the real world with your own eyes.

1. 下線部(1)の語を適切な形に変えなさい。【語彙の知識】　　　　　　　　　　　(2点)

　　　　　　　　　　　　　　　　　　　　　　　　　　

2. 下線部(2)は何を指していますか。英語で答えなさい。【内容についての思考力・判断力・表現力】 (3点)

　　　　　　　　　　　　　　　　　　　　　　　　　　

3. 空所(3)に入る最も適当な語(句)を選びなさい。【語彙と表現の知識】　　　　　(2点)

　　ア. As a result　　　イ. For example　　ウ. In other words　　エ. However

4. 下線部(4)の( )内の語句を適切に並べかえなさい。【表現の知識】　　　　　(3点)

　　　　　　　　　　　　　　　　　　　　　　　　　　

5. 空所(5)に入る最も適当な語(句)を選びなさい。【語彙の知識】　　　　　　　(2点)

　　ア. use　　　　　　イ. using　　　　　ウ. don't use　　　　エ. to use

6. 次の問いに英語で答えなさい。【内容についての思考力・判断力・表現力】　　　　　(各4点)

　　(1) What shouldn't you post when you use social media?

　　　　　　　　　　　　　　　　　　　　　　　　　　

　　(2) What should you do to look at the real world with your own eyes?

A Translate the English into Japanese and the Japanese into English.【語彙の知識】(各1点)

1. .... 形 A2　最近の　　　　　　2. event 名 A1　　　　　[　　　　　　]

3. .... 形 A1　毎日の　　　　　　4. discussion 名 A2　[　　　　　　]

5. .... 形 B1　巨大な　　　　　　6. .... 名 B1　手のひら

B Choose the word which has primary stress on a different syllable from the other three.【アクセントの知識】

(各2点)

1. ア. e-vent　　　　イ. prob-lem　　　ウ. re-cent　　　エ. so-cial

2. ア. fa-vor-ite　　イ. In-ter-net　　　ウ. in-tro-duce　　エ. won-der-ful

3. ア. at-ten-tion　イ. care-ful-ly　　ウ. dis-cus-sion　エ. how-ev-er

C Complete the following English sentences to match the Japanese.【表現と文法の知識】

(各3点)

1. 当時，私は自分の部屋を弟と共有していました。

I (　　　　　　) my room (　　　　　　) my brother in those days.

2. 私は中国語を読めますが，まったく話せません。

I (　　　　　　) read Chinese, and (　　　　　　) speak it at all.

3. 私たちは手話を使ってお互いにコミュニケーションをとることができます。

We can (　　　　　　) (　　　　　　) each other in sign language.

D Arrange the words in the proper order to match the Japanese.【表現と文法の知識・技能】

(各3点)

1. お名前をお伺いしてもよろしいですか。

(have / I / may / your name)?

2. だれにも私たちの秘密を話してはいけないよ。

You (anybody / must / tell / not) our secret.

3. 私たちといっしょにお昼ごはんを食べに行きませんか。

(don't / go / out / why / you) for lunch with us?

E Read the following passage and answer the questions below.

How do you use social media? You can share recent events in your everyday life with your friends. You can also introduce your favorite shops and (1)(interested, interesting) Internet news.

On social media, you can (2) some social problems, too. Sometimes you may have an (3)(excited, exciting) discussion about such problems with your friends.

If you (4) social media carefully, they can be a wonderful tool. You can (5)(all / communicate / over / people / with) the world. Now, why don't you open up a huge new world in the palm of your hand?

1. 下線部(1), (3)の語のうちから適当なほうを選びなさい。【語彙の知識】　　　　(各2点)

   (1) (　　　　　　　)

   (3) (　　　　　　　)

2. 空所(2)に入る最も適当な語(句)を選びなさい。【語彙の知識】　　　　(2点)

   ア. talk about　　　イ. say about　　　ウ. speak　　　エ. tell

3. 空所(4)に入る最も適当な語(句)を選びなさい。【語彙と文法の知識】　　　　(3点)

   ア. use　　　　　　イ. do not use　　　ウ. will use　　　エ. will not use

4. 下線部(5)の(　　)内の語を適切に並べかえなさい。【表現の知識】　　　　(3点)

----

5. 次の問いに英語で答えなさい。【内容についての思考力・判断力・表現力】　　　　(各4点)

   (1) What can you share with your friends on social media?

----

   (2) What is important to use social media as a wonderful tool?

Lesson 2 I Was Drinking Chocolate! Part 1

/50

Ⓐ Translate the English into Japanese and the Japanese into English.【語彙の知識】(各1点)

1. _____ 動 A1 …を飲む

2. _____ 動 B1 …の味がする

3. ancient 形 A2 [   ]

4. bar 名 A2 [   ]

5. presentation 名 B1 [   ]

6. _____ 名 A2 スライド

Ⓑ Choose the word which has primary stress on a different syllable from the other three.【アクセントの知識】

(各2点)

1. ア. an-cient   イ. bam-boo   ウ. fa-ther   エ. wel-come

2. ア. choc-o-late   イ. his-to-ry   ウ. to-mor-row   エ. yes-ter-day

3. ア. ac-tu-al-ly   イ. dif-fi-cul-ty   ウ. pre-sen-ta-tion   エ. tel-e-vi-sion

Ⓒ Complete the following English sentences to match the Japanese.【表現と文法の知識】

(各3点)

1. この課題にいっしょに取り組みましょう。

   Let's (   ) (   ) this task together.

2. チョコレートケーキはいかがですか。

   (   ) (   ) (   ) some chocolate cake?

3. 昨日の夕方, ケンジは川沿いを歩いていました。

   Kenji (   ) (   ) along the river yesterday evening.

Ⓓ Arrange the words in the proper order to match the Japanese.【表現と文法の知識・技能】

(各3点)

1. 私たちは明日新製品のプレゼンテーションを行います。

   We are (a presentation / give / going / to) on a new product.

   .

   _____

2. ミキは今, 電話で話をしています。

   Miki (is / on / talking / the phone) now.

   _____

3. お母さんが帰ってきたとき, あなたは何をしていましたか。

   (doing / were / what / you) when your mother came home?

   _____

E Read the following passage and answer the questions below.

> *Vivian:* Hello, Kumi!
>
> *Kumi:* Hi, Vivian! Welcome to my house. Come (1)!
>
> *Vivian:* Thank you. What were you doing, Kumi?
>
> *Kumi:* I was drinking chocolate.
>
> *Vivian:* Oh, I like hot chocolate! It really tastes good!
>
> *Kumi:* Um … do you know about the long history of chocolate?
>
> *Vivian:* I (2)(about / don't / much / know) it. Please tell me.
>
> *Kumi:* Actually, people drank chocolate from very ancient times. People first ate chocolate bars around 1850.
>
> *Vivian:* Is that right?
>
> *Kumi:* Yeah. Manabu and I are working (3) a project about the history of chocolate for an English class.
>
> *Vivian:* Are you going to give a presentation in class?
>
> *Kumi:* Yes. So (4)we have to make some good slides.

1. 空所(1), (3)に入る最も適当な語を選びなさい。【表現の知識】　　　　　　　　（各2点）

　　(1) ア. at　　　　　イ. from　　　　　ウ. in　　　　　エ. off

　　(3) ア. as　　　　　イ. into　　　　　ウ. on　　　　　エ. with

2. 下線部(2)の ( )内の語を適切に並べかえなさい。【表現と文法の知識】　　　　（4点）

　　..

3. 下線部(4)を日本語にしなさい。【語彙と表現の知識】　　　　　　　　　　　（4点）

　　..

4. 次の問いに英語で答えなさい。【内容についての思考力・判断力・表現力】　　　（各4点）

　　(1) What was Kumi doing when Vivian came to her house?

　　..

　　(2) Did people eat chocolate bars from very ancient times?

　　..

A Translate the English into Japanese and the Japanese into English. 【語彙の知識】(各1点)

1. .... 形 A2　野生の
2. cacao 名　[　　　　　]
3. grow 動 A1　[　　　　　]
4. .... 名 B1　税, 税金
5. .... 形 B1　固形の
6. precious 形 B1　[　　　　　]

B Choose the word which has primary stress on a different syllable from the other three. 【アクセントの知識】(各2点)

1. ア. a-broad　　イ. ba-by　　ウ. cen-tral　　エ. pan-da
2. ア. e-vent　　イ. gath-er　　ウ. im-age　　エ. yel-low
3. ア. ca-ca-o　　イ. dan-ger-ous　　ウ. Eng-lish-man　　エ. fi-nal-ly

C Complete the following English sentences to match the Japanese. 【表現と文法の知識】(各3点)

1. 新しいコンピュータを買いたいです。どれがおすすめですか。

I (　　　　　) (　　　　　) buy a new computer. Which do you recommend?

2. この店は11月27日から12月4日までメンテナンスのために休業します。

This shop will be closed for maintenance (　　　　　) November 27 (　　　　　) December 4.

3. 私はヴィヴィアンのことを親友の一人だと思っています。

I (　　　　　) of Vivian (　　　　　) one of my best friends.

D Arrange the words in the proper order to match the Japanese. 【表現と文法の知識・技能】(各3点)

1. 彼はコートのポケットに手を入れた。

He (his coat pocket / his hands / into / put).

2. 兄は何か食べるものを買いに出かけた。

My brother went out (eat / get / something / to / to).

3. 私たちはジムにそのニュースを伝えるために電話をした。

We (called Jim / him / tell / to) the news.

E Read the following passage and answer the questions below.

Kumi: Today, we want to talk about the history of chocolate. Over 3,000 years ago, people in Central America first had wild cacao beans. People there started (1)(grow) cacao trees.

Manabu: From about 250 to 900 AD, the Maya used wild cacao beans as money. (2)They used them in events for the gods, too. Cacao beans were very precious.

Kumi: From about 1200 to 1500, the Aztecs used cacao beans to pay taxes. In the 16th century, people in Spain found (3)this: Chocolate is good for people's health.

Manabu: They (4)(into / put / sugar and milk / the chocolate drink). It tasted good. Then, an Englishman made the first solid chocolate around 1850.

1. 下線部(1)の語を適切な形に変えなさい。【文法の知識】 (2点)

   ....

2. 下線部(2)を，They と them の内容を明らかにして日本語にしなさい。
   【内容についての思考力・判断力・表現力】 (4点)

   ....

   ....

3. 下線部(3)は何を指していますか。日本語で答えなさい。【内容についての思考力・判断力・表現力】
   (3点)

   ....

   ....

4. 下線部(4)の( )内の語句を適切に並べかえなさい。【表現の知識】 (3点)

   ....

5. 次の問いに英語で答えなさい。【内容についての思考力・判断力・表現力】 (各4点)
   (1) How did the Aztecs use cacao beans from about 1200 to 1500?

   ....

   (2) Who created a solid chocolate first?

   ....

Lesson 2 — I Was Drinking Chocolate!

Part 3

/50

A Translate the English into Japanese and the Japanese into English.【語彙の知識】(各1点)

1. .... 名 A1 誕生, 出生　　　　2. marriage 名 B1 　　[　　　　　　]

3. .... 名 A2 死　　　　　　　　4. .... 動 A2 …を捧げる

5. medicine 名 A1 　[　　　　　]　　6. recommend 動 B1 　[　　　　　　]

B Choose the word whose underlined part is pronounced differently from the other three.【発音の知識】(各2点)

1. ア. cli<u>mb</u>　　　　イ. <u>n</u>ice　　　　ウ. <u>s</u>ick　　　　エ. <u>s</u>lide

2. ア. <u>bea</u>n　　　　イ. <u>ce</u>remony　　ウ. <u>hea</u>lth　　エ. r<u>e</u>commend

3. ア. <u>a</u>ctually　　イ. <u>ma</u>rriage　　ウ. pre<u>se</u>ntation　エ. <u>ta</u>x

C Complete the following English sentences to match the Japanese.【表現と文法の知識】

(各3点)

1. そのお金は何のために使うのですか。

(　　　　　　) will you use that money (　　　　　　)?

2. 彼女はウェディングプランナーとして働いている。

She works (　　　　　) a wedding planner.

3. イタリアンレストランに行くのはどうですか。

(　　　　　) (　　　　　) (　　　　　　) to an Italian restaurant?

D Arrange the words in the proper order to match the Japanese.【表現と文法の知識・技能】

(各3点)

1. 父は週末ゴルフをして楽しみます。

My father (enjoys / golf / on / playing) weekends.

2. ピーターに私たちのハワイに行く計画について言わないでください。

Don't (about / our plan / Peter / tell) to go to Hawaii.

3. 散歩をすることは健康にいいですよ。

(a walk / good / is / taking) for your health.

E Read the following passage and answer the questions below.

> *Kumi:* Now, we want to hear your questions about our presentation.
>
> *Takashi:* What events (1)(cacao beans / did / for / the Maya / use)?
>
> *Manabu:* For their birth, marriage and death ceremonies. People offered cacao beans to the gods.
>
> *Taro:* Is chocolate really good for our health? Can you tell us more about this?
>
> *Kumi:* People in Spain drank chocolate as a health food. Sick people took (2)it as medicine. Um … (　3　)?
>
> *Vivian:* I want to buy some nice chocolate for my host mother. What do you recommend?
>
> *Kumi:* How about (4)(get) 100% cacao chocolate? It's not so sweet, but it's very healthy!

1. 下線部(1)の(　　)内の語句を適切に並べかえなさい。【表現の知識】　　　　　　　　(4点)

----

2. 下線部(2)は具体的には何を指していますか。英語1語で答えなさい。

【内容についての思考力・判断力・表現力】　(3点)

　　(　　　　　　　　)

3. 空所(3)に入るものとして適当でないものを選びなさい。【内容についての思考力・判断力・表現力】

(2点)

　ア. any ideas　　　イ. any other questions　　　ウ. anything else

4. 下線部(4)の語を適切な形に変えなさい。【文法の知識】　　　　　　　　　　　　(3点)

----

5. 次の問いに英語で答えなさい。【内容についての思考力・判断力・表現力】　　　(各4点)

(1) What did the Maya offer to the gods?

----

(2) How does 100% cacao chocolate taste?

A Translate the English into Japanese and the Japanese into English.【語彙の知識】(各 1 点)

1. develop 動 A2 [   ] 2. .... 名 A2 競技会，試合

3. .... 名 A2 賞   4. hardship 名 B1 [   ]

5. .... 動 B1 苦しむ   6. trust 動 A2 [   ]

B Choose the word which has primary stress on a different syllable from the other three.【アクセントの知識】

(各 2 点)

1. ア. a-ward   イ. fig-ure   ウ. hard-ship   エ. med-al

2. ア. de-vel-op   イ. how-ev-er   ウ. in-ju-ry   エ. O-lym-pic

3. ア. com-pe-ti-tion   イ. in-for-ma-tion   ウ. in-spi-ra-tion   エ. mem-o-ra-ble

C Complete the following English sentences to match the Japanese.【表現と文法の知識】

(各 3 点)

1. 彼女は最初はそのニュースを信じなかった。

She didn't believe the news (   ) (   ).

2. 私の父がフットボールのスター選手であったことを知っていますか。

Do you (   ) (   ) my father was a football star?

3. 私は午後からも一生懸命勉強し続けるつもりだ。

I will keep studying hard from the afternoon (   ) (   ).

D Arrange the words in the proper order to match the Japanese.【表現と文法の知識・技能】

(各 3 点)

1. 私は，彼がその仕事に最適な人だと思います。

I think (is / he / that / the best person) for the work.

_____

2. トムはその演技で主演男優賞を受賞した。

Tom (for / his performance / the best actor award / won).

_____

3. 両親が私を愛してくれていることはわかっています。

I know (love / me / my parents / that).

_____

E Read the following passage and answer the questions below.

Yuzuru Hanyu started skating in Sendai when he was four. (1) first, he didn't like practicing, but he loved (2)(show) people his figure skating skills. He developed his skills and won international junior competitions in 2009.

After that, Yuzuru won memorable medals and awards. His second Olympic gold was the 1,000th gold in the Winter Olympics. He (3)(give) the People's Honor Award in 2018.

Yuzuru (4)(as / faced / many hardships / well). After the 2014 Olympics, he suffered several injuries. He even injured his ankle shortly before the 2018 Olympics. (5), he trusted himself and always thought about skating. Yuzuru thought that those hardships gave him the power to win.

1. 空所(1)に入る最も適当な語を選びなさい。【表現の知識】 (2点)

　　ア. At　　　　　イ. For　　　　ウ. In　　　　エ. On

2. 下線部(2), (3)の語を適切な形に変えなさい。【文法の知識】 (各2点)

　　(2) ....

　　(3) ....

3. 下線部(4)の( )内の語句を適切に並べかえなさい。【表現の知識】 (3点)

....

4. 空所(5)に入る最も適当な語(句)を選びなさい。【語彙と表現の知識】 (3点)

　　ア. As a result　　イ. Besides　　ウ. However　　エ. Thus

5. 次の問いに英語で答えなさい。【内容についての思考力・判断力・表現力】 (各4点)

　　(1) What did Yuzuru win in 2009?

....

　　(2) What happened to Yuzuru shortly before the 2018 Olympics?

....

Inspiration on the Ice

Part 2

/50

A Translate the English into Japanese and the Japanese into English.【語彙の知識】(各1点)

1. rink 名 [   ]

2. ＿＿＿＿＿＿ 動 B1 逃げる

3. arena 名 B2 [   ]

4. ＿＿＿＿＿＿ 名 B1 災害

5. parade 動 [   ]

6. ＿＿＿＿＿＿ 動 A1 …を歓迎する

B Choose the word which has primary stress on a different syllable from the other three.【アクセントの知識】 (各2点)

1. ア. an-kle イ. earth-quake ウ. es-cape エ. hon-or

2. ア. pa-rade イ. re-turn ウ. sup-port エ. wel-come

3. ア. an-oth-er イ. a-re-na ウ. char-i-ty エ. dis-as-ter

C Complete the following English sentences to match the Japanese.【表現の知識】 (各3点)

1. その男性は燃えさかる車から脱出した。

 The man (   ) (   ) the burning car.

2. 彼の目的は被災地の住民たちを元気づけることだった。

 His purpose was to cheer up the people in the (   ) areas.

3. 兄は昨夜遅くに帰ってきた。

 My brother (   ) (   ) late last night.

D Arrange the words in the proper order to match the Japanese.【表現と文法の知識・技能】

(各3点)

1. お元気そうで何よりです。

 I (happy / that / to / know / am) you are fine.

2. こんなに勇気の出る言葉を聞いたことがない。

 I (have / heard / never / such) encouraging words.

3. もうその動画を見ましたか。

 Have (the video / watched / yet / you)?

E Read the following passage and answer the questions below.

The Great East Japan Earthquake in 2011 was another hardship for Yuzuru. He (1)(be) training at his home rink at the time. Yuzuru escaped from the arena. Ten days later, he started skating again with the help of people around him.

Since then, Yuzuru (2)(about / has / people in disaster areas / thought). He has (3)(skate) in a lot of charity ice shows. When he (4)(win) his first Olympic gold, he said, "I'm here (5) many people around the world have supported me."

After the 2018 Olympics, Yuzuru paraded through the streets of Sendai. About (6)100,000 people welcomed him. "I'm happy to come back here with this gold medal," Yuzuru said during the ceremony.

1. 下線部(1)，(3)，(4)の語を適切な形に変えなさい。【文法の知識】　　　(各2点)

   (1) _____

   (3) _____

   (4) _____

2. 下線部(2)の(　　)内の語句を適切に並べかえなさい。【表現と文法の知識】　　　(2点)

_____

3. 空所(5)に入る最も適当な語を選びなさい。【語彙の知識】　　　(2点)

   ア．although　　　イ．because　　　ウ．that　　　　　エ．when

4. 下線部(6)を英語で書き表しなさい。【表現の知識】　　　(2点)

_____

5. 次の問いに英語で答えなさい。【内容についての思考力・判断力・表現力】　　　(各4点)

  (1) Why was Yuzuru able to start skating again just ten days after the earthquake?

_____

  (2) Where did Yuzuru parade after the 2018 Olympics?

_____

Lesson 3 — Inspiration on the Ice — Part 3 — /50

A Translate the English into Japanese and the Japanese into English. 【語彙の知識】(各1点)

1. _____ 名 A2 友情
2. _____ 動 B1 競う，競争する
3. weep 動 [   ]
4. train 動 A2 [   ]
5. _____ 形 B1 誇りに思う
6. inspire 動 B1 [   ]

B Choose the word whose underlined part is pronounced differently from the other three. 【発音の知識】 (各2点)

1. ア. comp<u>e</u>te   イ. dev<u>e</u>lop   ウ. m<u>e</u>dal   エ. w<u>e</u>pt
2. ア. <u>i</u>njury   イ. <u>i</u>nspire   ウ. pr<u>i</u>vate   エ. s<u>i</u>lent
3. ア. ar<u>ou</u>nd   イ. cl<u>ou</u>d   ウ. pr<u>ou</u>d   エ. thr<u>ou</u>gh

C Complete the following English sentences to match the Japanese. 【表現の知識】 (各3点)

1. 彼女はクラスメイトの前で突然泣き出した。

   She suddenly started to cry (   ) (   ) of her classmates.

2. 今の天気はどんな感じですか。

   (   ) is the weather like now?

3. 彼はあきらめなかったので，私は彼のことを誇りに思う。

   He didn't give up, so I'm (   ) (   ) him.

D Arrange the words in the proper order to match the Japanese. 【表現と文法の知識・技能】

(各3点)

1. 今日，スマートフォンは世界中で使われている。

   Today, (all / are / over / smartphones / used) the world.

   _____

2. うちの子は公園に一人で行くには幼すぎる。

   My kid (go / is / to / too / young) to the park alone.

   _____

3. 試合後，その選手たちはお互いに握手をした。

   The players (each / hands / other / shook / with) after the match.

   _____

E Read the following passage and answer the questions below.

Reporter: I'd (1)(about / ask / like / to / you) your friendship with Javier Fernandez.

Yuzuru: Thank you. I'm glad to talk about Javier because I know he is often (2)(ask) about me by Japanese reporters.

Reporter: What's he like?

Yuzuru: He's very kind. (3) kind to compete, I think. I won the gold medal at the Olympics, and he (4)(   ) third place. I wept. We trained together, and I knew he worked hard to get a medal. I was proud (5) him.

Reporter: What does he mean to you?

Yuzuru: He means a lot to me. We've always inspired each other. I got the gold because he's been with me.

1. 下線部(1)の(   )内の語を適切に並べかえなさい。【表現の知識】 (3点)

....

2. 下線部(2)の語を適切な形に変えなさい。【文法の知識】 (2点)

....

3. 空所(3), (5)に入る最も適当な語を選びなさい。【語彙と表現の知識】 (各2点)

(3) ア. As   イ. So   ウ. Such   エ. Too
(5) ア. for   イ. in   ウ. of   エ. with

4. 下線部(4)が「3位になった」という意味になるように, (   )に入る最も適当な語を選びなさい。【表現の知識】 (3点)

ア. caught   イ. had   ウ. took   エ. went

5. 次の問いに英語で答えなさい。【内容についての思考力・判断力・表現力】 (各4点)

(1) According to Yuzuru, what is Javier like?

....

(2) What did Yuzuru get thanks to Javier?

....

A Translate the English into Japanese and the Japanese into English.【語彙の知識】(各1点)

1. individual 形 B1　[　　　　　] 2. ＿＿＿＿＿＿ 動 B1 進歩する

3. gamer 名　[　　　　　] 4. ＿＿＿＿＿＿ 形 B2 上手な，熟練した

5. ＿＿＿＿＿＿ 名 B1 組織，団体 6. gaming 名　[　　　　　]

B Choose the word which has primary stress on a different syllable from the other three.【アクセントの知識】　(各2点)

1. ア. ad-vance 　　イ. ap-pear 　　ウ. friend-ship 　　エ. sup-port

2. ア. at-ten-tion 　イ. dif-fi-cult 　ウ. fa-vor-ite 　　エ. pop-u-lar

3. ア. com-mu-ni-cate 　イ. dic-tion-ar-y 　ウ. pro-fes-sion-al 　エ. tech-nol-o-gy

C Complete the following English sentences to match the Japanese.【表現と文法の知識】

(各3点)

1. 私は単なる楽しみのためにフランス語を勉強し始めた。

I started to study French just (　　　　　) (　　　　　).

2. 兄は父よりも背が高い。

My elder brother is (　　　　　) (　　　　　) my father.

3. 昨日の夜，私はにわか雨にあった。その結果，風邪をひいた。

I was caught in a shower last night. (　　　　　) a (　　　　　), I've gotten a cold.

D Arrange the words in the proper order to match the Japanese.【表現と文法の知識・技能】

(各3点)

1. 今日では人々は携帯電話をさまざまな方法で使っています。

Today, people (cellphones / in / use / various / ways).

2. 太郎と競える人はいない。

(can / compete / nobody / with) Taro.

3. 私はその店でいちばん安いコンピュータを買った。

I (bought / computer / cheapest / the) in the store.

E Read the following passage and answer the questions below.

There is a popular, new sport today: esports. Esports is the short name for "electronic sports." Esports players play video games in individual or team competitions.

In the late 20th century, people (1)(start) playing video games for fun. Today, many people enjoy them (2) a different way. Computers and other machines today are (3)(smart) and cheaper than those of the 20th century. (4)Also, Internet technology has advanced, so people can now compete online with gamers around the world. They often use their own powerful machines.

Many players have become very skilled, and (5)(players / have / appeared / even / professional). Many organizations have started tournaments. As a result, such video gaming has gotten the name "esports."

1. 下線部(1), (3)の語を適切な形に変えなさい。【文法の知識】　　　　　　　（各2点）

(1) ....

(3) ....

2. 空所(2)に入る最も適当な語を選びなさい。【表現の知識】　　　　　　　　　（2点）

ア. at　　　　　　イ. by　　　　　　ウ. for　　　　　　エ. in

3. 下線部(4)を日本語にしなさい。【表現と文法の知識】　　　　　　　　　　　（3点）

....

....

4. 下線部(5)が「プロの選手すら現れるようになった」という意味になるように, (　　)内の語を適切に並べかえなさい。【表現と文法の知識】　　　　　　　　　　　　　　（3点）

....

5. 次の問いに英語で答えなさい。【内容についての思考力・判断力・表現力】　　　（各4点）

(1) What is the name of a popular, new sport?

....

(2) What do people use when they compete online with gamers around the world?

....

A Translate the English into Japanese and the Japanese into English. 【語彙の知識】(各1点)

1. various 形 B1　　[　　　　　　]　　2. _____ 名 B1　戦闘，対戦

3. respond 動 B1　　[　　　　　　]　　4. strategy 名 A2　　[　　　　　　]

5. _____ 名 A2　社会，世間　　　　　6. _____ 名 A2　基本，原理

B Choose the word whose underlined part is pronounced differently from the other three. 【発音の知識】

(各2点)

1. ア. b<u>a</u>sic　　　　イ. b<u>a</u>ttle　　　ウ. pr<u>a</u>ctice　　　エ. str<u>a</u>tegy

2. ア. an<u>o</u>ther　　　イ. g<u>o</u>ld　　　　ウ. <u>o</u>ver　　　　　エ. pr<u>o</u>gram

3. ア. el<u>e</u>ctronic　　イ. p<u>o</u>pular　　ウ. resp<u>o</u>nd　　　エ. s<u>o</u>ciety

C Complete the following English sentences to match the Japanese. 【表現と文法の知識】

(各3点)

1. そのテニスの試合は4月30日に開催されます。

The tennis tournament will (　　　　　　) (　　　　　　) on April 30.

2. 私は美術や音楽のような芸術系の教科が好きです。

I like artistic subjects (　　　　　　) (　　　　　　) art and music.

3. 近頃，ますます多くの人が東京を訪れている。

(　　　　　　) and (　　　　　　) people are visiting Tokyo these days.

D Arrange the words in the proper order to match the Japanese. 【表現と文法の知識・技能】

(各3点)

1. プロ野球選手になるのは有名な歌手になるのと同じくらい難しい。

Becoming a professional baseball player (as / as / becoming / difficult / is) a famous singer.

2. 私にこの機械の使い方を教えてください。

Please (teach / use / to / me / how) this machine.

3. 私の試験の結果は彼女ほどはよくなかった。

My exam results (as / as / good / hers / weren't).

E Read the following passage and answer the questions below.

Esports tournaments now take place online or in big arenas all over the world. (1)(against / compete / each / other / players) in various games, (2) battle games, card games and sports games.

(3)Becoming a great esports player is often (　　) (　　) (　　) becoming a great player of (　　) other (　　) of sport.　For example, players need to respond quickly and think hard about strategies.　They also need good communication skills because they often work as a team.

Today in Japan, more and more people believe that esports will change society. Some high schools have special programs for esports.　The students there learn the basics of IT and practice (4) to win games.

1. 下線部(1)の(　　)内の語を適切に並べかえなさい。【表現と文法の知識】　　　　　　　(4点)

2. 空所(2)に入る最も適当な語句を選びなさい。【表現の知識】　　　　　　　　　　　(3点)
　　ア. according to　　イ. because of　　ウ. in addition to　　エ. such as

3. 下線部(3)が「すぐれたeスポーツ選手になるのは，しばしば，他の種類のすぐれたスポーツ選手になるのと同じくらい難しい。」という意味になるように，(　　)に適語を補いなさい。
　　　　　　　　　　　　　　　　　　　　　　　　　　　　　　　　【表現と文法の知識】（完答3点）

Becoming a great esports player is often (　　　　　) (　　　　　) (　　　　　) becoming a great player of (　　　　　) other (　　　　　) of sport.

4. 空所(4)に入る最も適当な語を選びなさい。【表現と文法の知識】　　　　　　　　　(2点)
　　ア. how　　　　　イ. what　　　　　ウ. where　　　　　エ. which

5. 次の問いに英語で答えなさい。【内容についての思考力・判断力・表現力】　　　　　(各4点)
　　(1) What is held online or in big arenas all over the world?

　　(2) What do esports players need in order to work as a team?

Esports' Time Has Arrived

Part 3

/50

A Translate the English into Japanese and the Japanese into English. 【語彙の知識】(各 1 点)

1. waste 名 B1 [   ]　　2. following 形 A1 [   ]

3. ＿＿＿＿＿ 副 A2 身体的に，肉体的に　　4. mentally 副 B1 [   ]

5. ＿＿＿＿＿ 動 A2 …を向上させる　　6. ＿＿＿＿＿ 動 B1 …を養成する

B Choose the word which has primary stress on a different syllable from the other three. 【アクセントの知識】

(各 2 点)

1. ア. a-gainst　　イ. be-cause　　ウ. im-prove　　エ. kitch-en

2. ア. com-put-er　　イ. cul-ti-vate　　ウ. fol-low-ing　　エ. men-tal-ly

3. ア. char-i-ty　　イ. In-ter-net　　ウ. med-i-cine　　エ. un-der-stand

C Complete the following English sentences to match the Japanese. 【表現と文法の知識】

(各 3 点)

1. あなたに私といっしょに来てほしいです。

   I (   ) (   ) (   ) come with me.

2. 明日晴れたら，海に行きます。

   If it (   ) sunny tomorrow, I (   ) (   ) to
   the sea.

3. またあなたにお会いしたい。

   I (   ) (   ) see you again.

D Arrange the words in the proper order to match the Japanese. 【表現と文法の知識・技能】

(各 3 点)

1. 彼は私たちにこのコンピュータを修理するように言った。

   He (fix / to / told / us) this computer.

   ＿＿＿＿＿＿＿＿＿＿＿＿＿＿＿＿＿＿＿＿＿＿＿＿＿＿＿＿＿＿

2. 今朝，始発列車に乗るために早起きしました。

   I (catch / early / got / to / up) the first train this morning.

   ＿＿＿＿＿＿＿＿＿＿＿＿＿＿＿＿＿＿＿＿＿＿＿＿＿＿＿＿＿＿

3. テレビを見ることは時間の無駄だと思う。

   I think (a waste / is / of / time / TV / watching).

   ＿＿＿＿＿＿＿＿＿＿＿＿＿＿＿＿＿＿＿＿＿＿＿＿＿＿＿＿＿＿

E Read the following passage and answer the questions below.

I'm 15. I love esports. I hope to become a good esports player. (1)It's my future dream. But (2)my parents (become / don't / me / to / want) an esports player. They say playing computer games is only a waste of time. Am I wrong?

Answer

I live in South Korea. I'm working hard to become a professional esports player. You have the same dream, too, right? Then, learn the following things.

   1. Be strong and healthy — physically and (　3　).

   2. Improve your (　4　) skills — especially English skills.

   3. (5)Cultivate your spirit of fair play.

I know these are not easy. But if you work hard, your parents will understand you.

1. 下線部(1)は何を指していますか。英語で答えなさい。【内容についての思考力・判断力・表現力】(2点)

2. 下線部(2)が「私の両親は私にeスポーツ選手になってほしくないと思っている」という意味
　になるように，(　　)内の語を適切に並べかえなさい。【表現と文法の知識】　　　　(3点)

3. 空所(3)，(4)に入る最も適当な語を選びなさい。【語彙の知識，内容についての思考力・判断力・表現力】

　　　　　　　　　　　　　　　　　　　　　　　　　　　　　　　　　　　　　　(各2点)

   (3) ア. friendly　　　イ. mentally　　　ウ. nationally　　　エ. seriously

   (4) ア. computer　　イ. driving　　　ウ. language　　　エ. sports

4. 下線部(5)を日本語にしなさい。【語彙と表現の知識】　　　　　　　　　　　　　　(3点)

5. 次の問いに英語で答えなさい。【内容についての思考力・判断力・表現力】　　　　(各4点)

   (1) What do the boy's parents say about playing computer games?

   (2) What does the South Korean girl want to become?

A Translate the English into Japanese and the Japanese into English.【語彙の知識】(各1点)

1. .... 形　演劇の　　　　　2. .... 名 A1　息子

3. .... 動 A2　…のように思われる　　4. traditional 形 A2　[　　　　　]

5. awesome 形 B1　[　　　　　]　　6. sometime 副 B1　[　　　　　]

B Choose the word whose underlined part is pronounced differently from the other three.【発音の知識】(各2点)

1. ア. <u>a</u>lso　　　イ. <u>a</u>wesome　　ウ. p<u>o</u>ster　　エ. th<u>ou</u>ght

2. ア. <u>a</u>ctually　　イ. dis<u>a</u>ster　　ウ. f<u>a</u>mous　　エ. the<u>a</u>trical

3. ア. c<u>e</u>remony　　イ. comp<u>e</u>te　　ウ. dr<u>ea</u>m　　エ. s<u>ee</u>m

C Complete the following English sentences to match the Japanese.【表現と文法の知識】

(各3点)

1. あの泣いている赤ちゃんを見て。

　Look at that (　　　　　) (　　　　　).

2. 昼食後，先生たちは忙しそうだった。

　The teachers (　　　　　) (　　　　　) after lunch.

3. 彼女は英語がとても上手だ。そのうえ，韓国語も話せる。

　Her English is very good. (　　　　　) (　　　　　), she can speak Korean.

D Arrange the words in the proper order to match the Japanese.【表現と文法の知識・技能】

(各3点)

1. あそこで木に登っている男の子を知っていますか。

　Do you know (a tree / climbing / over / the boy) there?

2. パジャマを着た男性が駅のほうへ走っているよ。

　A man (is / pajamas / running / to / wearing) the station.

3. 彼女はまるで子供のようにふるまっていた。

　She was (a child / acting / just / like).

E Read the following passage and answer the questions below.

> *Kumi:* Look at this poster, Vivian.
>
> *Vivian:* Hmm … (1)<u>The man (a mask / dancing / is / wearing)</u>, and the two men are (2)(play) music.
>
> *Kumi:* Yeah. This poster was for a *Kyogen* performance in France.
>
> *Vivian:* I see. Then, who are Mansaku, Mansai, and Yuki Nomura?
>
> *Kumi:* They are famous *Kyogen* performers. Actually, they are a grandfather, a father, and a son.
>
> *Vivian:* Do you think I'll like watching *Kyogen*? The stories seem difficult for me.
>
> *Kumi:* (3) worry! The stories are simple and funny. (4), *Kyogen* has a traditional and beautiful style, just like *No*, *Kabuki*, and *Bunraku*.
>
> *Vivian:* Okay. Now, I want to learn more about *Kyogen*.
>
> *Kumi:* Awesome! Let's go to the theater sometime.
>
> *Vivian:* I can't wait!

1. 下線部(1)が「面をつけた男性が踊っている」という意味になるように，（　　）内の語句を適切に並べかえなさい。【表現と文法の知識】　　　　　　　　　　　　　　　　　　　　　　　　　　(3点)

　　　‥‥‥‥‥‥‥‥‥‥‥‥‥‥‥‥‥‥‥‥‥‥‥‥‥‥‥‥‥‥‥‥‥‥‥‥‥

2. 下線部(2)の語を適切な形に変えなさい。【文法の知識】　　　　　　　　　　(3点)

　　　‥‥‥‥‥‥‥‥‥‥‥‥‥‥‥‥‥‥‥‥‥‥‥‥‥‥‥‥‥‥‥‥‥‥‥‥‥

3. 空所(3)に入る最も適当な語を選びなさい。【文法の知識】　　　　　　　　　(3点)

　　ア. Be　　　　　　イ. Do　　　　　　ウ. Don't　　　　　エ. Not

4. 空所(4)に入る最も適当な語句を選びなさい。【表現の知識，内容についての思考力・判断力・表現力】(3点)

　　ア. As a result　　　イ. For example　　ウ. In addition　　エ. In contrast

5. 次の問いに英語で答えなさい。【内容についての思考力・判断力・表現力】　　　　　(各4点)

　　(1) Who is the father of Mansai Nomura?

　　　‥‥‥‥‥‥‥‥‥‥‥‥‥‥‥‥‥‥‥‥‥‥‥‥‥‥‥‥‥‥‥‥‥‥‥‥‥

　　(2) Did Vivian become interested in *Kyogen* after the conversation?

　　　‥‥‥‥‥‥‥‥‥‥‥‥‥‥‥‥‥‥‥‥‥‥‥‥‥‥‥‥‥‥‥‥‥‥‥‥‥

Lesson 5 — Mansai, *Kyogen* Performer — Part 2

/50

A Translate the English into Japanese and the Japanese into English.【語彙の知識】(各1点)

1. living 形 A1　[　　　　　　]　　2. treasure 名 A2　[　　　　　　]

3. ＿＿＿＿＿ 名 A2　世代　　　　4. ＿＿＿＿＿ 形 B1　厳しい

5. ＿＿＿＿＿ 動 A2　助言する　　6. attention 名 A2　[　　　　　　]

B Choose the word which has primary stress on a different syllable from the other three.【アクセントの知識】(各2点)

1. ア. ad-vise　　　イ. ap-pear　　ウ. pro-gram　　エ. se-vere

2. ア. ad-di-tion　　イ. at-ten-tion　ウ. dif-fi-cult　　エ. per-form-er

3. ア. com-mu-ni-cate　イ. gen-er-a-tion　ウ. the-at-ri-cal　エ. tra-di-tion-al

C Complete the following English sentences to match the Japanese.【表現と文法の知識】

(各3点)

1. 彼は俳優としても歌手としても有名だ。

He is famous (　　　　　) as an actor (　　　　　) as a singer.

2. 祖父は毎日ゆで卵を2個食べる。

My grandfather eats two (　　　　　) (　　　　　) every day.

3. 彼女は2度目の交通事故の後にたいへんな時期を経験した。

She (　　　　　) (　　　　　) a hard time after the second traffic accident.

D Arrange the words in the proper order to match the Japanese.【表現と文法の知識・技能】

(各3点)

1. 私は5歳のときに日本に引っ越してきました。

I moved to Japan (age / at / five / of / the).

2. 私たちはその川で捕れた魚を食べた。

We ate (caught / in / some fish / the river).

3. デイヴィッドは日本製のカメラが好きです。

David likes (cameras / in / Japan / made).

E Read the following passage and answer the questions below.

Mansai was born in 1966. His family (1) *Kyogen* since the Edo period. Both his father and grandfather are living national treasures. Mansai performed on stage for the first time at the age of three.

Kyogen is a traditional art (2) down from one generation to another. *Kyogen* performers go through severe training to learn the tradition. However, just being strict in traditional ways (3)(better / *Kyogen* / make / may / not).

Mansai believes he can perform *Kyogen* better by doing different things. (4), he studied Shakespeare's plays in London in 1994. He also acts in movies and appears on TV. He even advised Yuzuru Hanyu on his skating program, *SEIMEI*. In this way, Mansai has (5)(draw) people's attention to *Kyogen*.

1. 空所(1), (2)に入る最も適当な語(句)を選びなさい。【文法の知識】　　　　　(各2点)

   (1) ア. has performed　　イ. performed　　ウ. performing　　エ. to perform

   (2) ア. pass　　　　　　　イ. passed　　　　ウ. passes　　　　エ. passing

2. 下線部(3)の(　　　)内の語を適切に並べかえなさい。【表現と文法の知識】　　　(3点)

   ....

3. 空所(4)に入る最も適当な語(句)を選びなさい。【語彙と表現の知識, 内容についての思考力・判断力・表現力】

   (3点)

   ア. For example　　イ. However　　　ウ. In other words　　エ. Moreover

4. 下線部(5)の語を適切な形に変えなさい。【文法の知識】　　　　　　　　　　(2点)

   ....

5. 次の問いに英語で答えなさい。【内容についての思考力・判断力・表現力】　　　(各4点)

   (1) When did Mansai's family start to perform *Kyogen*?

   ....

   (2) Why did Mansai study Shakespeare's plays?

   ....

Mansai, *Kyogen* Performer

/50

A Translate the English into Japanese and the Japanese into English. 【語彙の知識】(各1点)

1. _____ 動 B1   …を含む   2. motion 名 B2   [   ]

3. adviser 名 B1   [   ]   4. fusion 名   [   ]

5. classical 形 B1   [   ]   6. _____ 形 A2   現代の, 近代の

B Choose the word which has primary stress on a different syllable from the other three. 【アクセントの知識】   (各2点)

1. ア. in-volve   イ. mod-ern   ウ. mo-tion   エ. fu-sion

2. ア. ad-vis-er   イ. clas-si-cal   ウ. dig-it-al   エ. his-to-ry

3. ア. Par-a-lym-pics   イ. en-vi-ron-ment   ウ. tech-nol-o-gy   エ. sur-pris-ing-ly

C Complete the following English sentences to match the Japanese. 【表現と文法の知識】

(各3点)

1. ポールはその映画で大統領の役を演じた。

   Paul (   ) the (   ) of the president in the movie.

2. 冬にあの山に登るのは危険だ。

   It (   ) dangerous (   ) (   ) that mountain in winter.

3. 彼は昨日外出できなかった。宿題をしないといけなかったから。

   He couldn't go out yesterday. That (   ) (   ) he had to do his homework.

D Arrange the words in the proper order to match the Japanese. 【表現と文法の知識・技能】

(各3点)

1. 彼女にとってその質問に答えるのはとても難しかった。

   It was (answer / for / her / to / very difficult) the question.

   _____

2. 黄色を青と混ぜると緑になる。

   (if / mix / with / yellow / you) blue, you get green.

   _____

3. 妹は去年リレーの選手に選ばれた。

   My sister (a relay runner / as / chosen / was) last year.

   _____

E Read the following passage and answer the questions below.

One of Mansai's new efforts involved digital technology. He performed （ 1 ）
a motion capture actor for the movie *Shin Godzilla* in 2016.   It (2)(easy / for /
Mansai / play / to / was) the role of Godzilla. He moved in the *Kyogen* style! "I'm
glad that *Kyogen*'s history of more than 650 years is (3)(mix) with the DNA of
Godzilla," Mansai said.

   Mansai was (4)(choose) as the adviser of the opening and closing ceremonies
of the Tokyo Olympics and Paralympics. This was because he worked on the
fusion of classical art and modern theater. Mansai's goal is (5)(a bridge / on /
pass / to / to become) (6)the traditional art to the next generation.

1. 空所(1)に入る最も適当な語を選びなさい。【語彙と表現の知識】　　　　　　　　　　（2点）

   ア. as　　　　　　イ. in　　　　　　ウ. of　　　　　　エ. to

2. 下線部(2), (5)の（　　）内の語句を適切に並べかえなさい。【表現と文法の知識】　　　（各2点）

   (2) _____

   (5) _____

3. 下線部(3), (4)の語を適切な形に変えなさい。【文法の知識】　　　　　　　　　　（各2点）

   (3) _____

   (4) _____

4. 下線部(6)は具体的には何を指していますか。英語1語で答えなさい。

【内容についての思考力・判断力・表現力】　（2点）

   (　　　　　　　　)

5. 次の問いに英語で答えなさい。【内容についての思考力・判断力・表現力】　　　　　　（各4点）

   (1) How did Mansai move when he performed as a motion capture actor for
   Shin Godzilla?

   _____

   (2) Why was Mansai chosen as the adviser of the opening and closing
   ceremonies of the Tokyo Olympics and Paralympics?

   _____

In this Corner of the World Part 1

/50

A Translate the English into Japanese and the Japanese into English.【語彙の知識】(各1点)

1. production 名 A2　[　　　　　　　　] 　　2. _____ 動 B2　…を寄付する

3. ordinary 形 B1　[　　　　　　　　] 　　4. _____ 動 B2　興味を引く, 訴える

5. _____ 動 B1　…を魅了する　　6. viewer 名 B2　[　　　　　　　]

B Choose the word which has primary stress on a different syllable from the other three.【アクセントの知識】　　(各2点)

1. ア. earth-quake　　イ. gath-er　　ウ. rea-son　　エ. re-view

2. ア. ap-peal　　イ. at-tract　　ウ. e-nough　　エ. view-er

3. ア. beau-ti-ful-ly　イ. ma-te-ri-al　ウ. or-di-nar-y　エ. u-su-al-ly

C Complete the following English sentences to match the Japanese.【表現と文法の知識】

(各3点)

1. 彼女はこれまでに100冊以上の小説を読みました。

She has read (　　　　　) (　　　　　) 100 novels so far.

2. 私は娘に幸せな生活を送ってほしいと思っています。

I hope that my daughter (　　　　　) a happy (　　　　　).

3. 医者に診てもらうために長時間待っています。

I've (　　　　　) (　　　　　) to see the doctor for a long time.

D Arrange the words in the proper order to match the Japanese.【表現と文法の知識・技能】

(各3点)

1. ますます多くの人々がパーティーに参加したがっている。

(and / more / more / people / want) to join the party.

_____

2. これはかなり高価なコンピュータです。

This is (an / computer / expensive / quite).

_____

3. トムは5時間テレビゲームをしています。

Tom (a video game / been / has / playing) for five hours.

_____

E Read the following passage and answer the questions below.

A lot of people helped to make the movie *In this Corner of the World*. When the movie project started, there was not enough money. (1)The production staff asked people to donate money on the Internet. Surprisingly, the staff gathered about 40 million yen (2) more than 3,000 people.

The movie became a hit. One of the reasons for this was the power of social media. Good reviews spread, and more and more people went to see (3)it.

Another reason was that the movie shows the real life of a family during World War II. The family members (4)(an / led / life / ordinary / quite), just as we do. That appealed strongly (5) a lot of people. Ever since the movie came out, it has been attracting many viewers.

1. 下線部(1)を日本語にしなさい。【表現と文法の知識】 (3点)

_____

2. 空所(2), (5)に入る最も適当な語を選びなさい。【語彙と表現の知識】 (各2点)
　　(2) ア. by　　　　イ. from　　　　ウ. on　　　　エ. with
　　(5) ア. at　　　　イ. in　　　　ウ. on　　　　エ. to

3. 下線部(3)が指すものを，本文中から2語で抜き出しなさい。【内容についての思考力・判断力・表現力】 (2点)

　　(　　　　　　) (　　　　　　　　)

4. 下線部(4)の (　　　) 内の語を適切に並べかえなさい。【表現の知識】 (3点)

_____

5. 次の問いに英語で答えなさい。【内容についての思考力・判断力・表現力】 (各4点)
　　(1) How much money did the movie production staff gather?

　　_____

　　(2) What made good reviews spread?

　　_____

A Translate the English into Japanese and the Japanese into English.【語彙の知識】(各1点)

1. ＿＿＿＿＿＿ 名 A2 方法　　　　　　2. invent 動 A2 [　　　　　　]

3. ＿＿＿＿＿＿ 名 B1 量　　　　　　　4. ＿＿＿＿＿＿ 形 A2 軍の

5. search 動 B1 [　　　　　　]　　　6. burst 動 B1 [　　　　　　]

B Choose the word whose underlined part is pronounced differently from the other three.【発音の知識】(各2点)

1. ア. h<u>i</u>ll　　　　イ. <u>i</u>nvent　　　ウ. m<u>i</u>litary　　　エ. s<u>i</u>gn

2. ア. b<u>a</u>ttleship　イ. d<u>ay</u>　　　　ウ. f<u>a</u>mous　　　エ. gr<u>ea</u>t

3. ア. f<u>igh</u>t　　　　イ. l<u>augh</u>ter　　ウ. strai<u>gh</u>t　　　エ. thou<u>gh</u>

C Complete the following English sentences to match the Japanese.【表現と文法の知識】

(各3点)

1. このプロジェクトは資金が不足してきている。

This project is running (　　　　　　) (　　　　　　) money.

2. 彼女はいつも私に答えにくい質問をする。

She always asks me questions (　　　　　　) (　　　　　　) difficult to answer.

3. ジェーンは鍵を見つけようとバッグの中を捜した。

Jane (　　　　　　) her bag (　　　　　　) the key.

D Arrange the words in the proper order to match the Japanese.【表現と文法の知識・技能】

(各3点)

1. 外国での新しい生活にすぐに慣れるでしょう。

You'll soon (a new life / get / to / used) in a foreign country.

2. 私には写真家の友人がいます。

I have (a friend / a photographer / is / who).

3. 彼はとても悲しかったので何も食べられませんでした。

He was (couldn't / he / sad / so / that) eat anything.

E Read the following passage and answer the questions below.

The main character Suzu gets (1)(marry) to Shusaku and moves from Hiroshima to Kure. She tries hard to get used to the new environment.

(2) time passes, people are running short of food. Suzu cooks meals by (3)(use) wild plants. One day, when she cooks, (4)she uses (by / that / was / a method / invented) a famous samurai and increases the amount of food.

Suzu likes drawing pictures. One day, when she draws a picture of battleships on a hill, the military police suspect her (5) spying. They search her house for some signs of spying. The people in her family try hard not to laugh because Suzu is so absent-minded that she can never spy! They (6)(　　)(　　) laughter after the police leave.

1. 下線部(1), (3)の語を適切な形に変えなさい。【表現と文法の知識】　　　　(各2点)

    (1) ....

    (3) ....

2. 空所(2), (5)に入る最も適当な語を選びなさい。【語彙と表現の知識】　　　(各2点)

    (2) ア. After　　　　イ. As　　　　ウ. Since　　　　エ. When

    (5) ア. about　　　　イ. from　　　　ウ. in　　　　エ. of

3. 下線部(4)が「彼女はある有名な侍が考案した方法を使う」という意味になるように, (　　) 内の語句を適切に並べかえなさい。【表現と文法の知識】　　　　(2点)

    ....

4. 下線部(6)が「突然笑い出す」という意味になるように, (　　)に適語を補いなさい。【表現の知識】

    (　　　　　　　)(　　　　　　　　)　　　　　　　　　　　　　　(2点)

5. 次の問いに英語で答えなさい。【内容についての思考力・判断力・表現力】　　　(各4点)

    (1) What did Suzu use when she cooked meals?

    ....

    (2) Was Suzu a spy?

    ....

A Translate the English into Japanese and the Japanese into English. 【語彙の知識】（各1点）

1. chat 名 B1 [   ]   2. fateful 形 [   ]

3. _____ 動 A1 …を推測する   4. _____ 副 A2 どこかへ

5. path 名 A2 [   ]   6. _____ 名 B1 決断

B Choose the word which has primary stress on a different syllable from the other three. 【アクセントの知識】 （各2点）

1. ア. fate-ful   イ. im-prove   ウ. meth-od   エ. some-where

2. ア. char-ac-ter   イ. de-ci-sion   ウ. how-ev-er   エ. tra-di-tion

3. ア. cul-tur-al   イ. In-ter-net   ウ. pro-duc-tion   エ. the-a-ter

C Complete the following English sentences to match the Japanese. 【表現と文法の知識】

（各3点）

1. 今日中にこの宿題を終えなければならない。

   I (   ) (   ) finish this homework today.

2. 会議をするのにどこかいいところを知りませんか。

   Do you know (   ) nice for a meeting?

3. 夜中に突然目が覚めて，それきり寝つけなかった。

   I suddenly (   ) (   ) in the night and couldn't go back to sleep.

D Arrange the words in the proper order to match the Japanese. 【表現と文法の知識・技能】

（各3点）

1. それはトムがこの間私にしたのと同じ話です。

   It's the same story (which / me / Tom / told) the other day.

_____

2. あなたが買ってくれた本をなくしてしまいました。

   I've lost (bought / for / me / the book / you).

_____

3. 祖父は今の自分に誇りを持っている。

   My grandfather is (he / is / of / proud / who) now.

_____

E Read the following passage and answer the questions below.

Shusaku asks Suzu to come to his office (1)(*a notebook / forgot / he / which / with*). *Actually, he wants to talk with her.* (2) *a bridge, they are* (3)*having a chat about their fateful meeting and married life.*

Suzu: I guess I'm just afraid I'll wake up from a dream.
Shusaku: Dream?
Suzu: (4)(Have) to change my name and move somewhere new was hard for me, but you've been so kind, and I've made friends. I don't want to wake up because I'm really happy to be who I (5)(be) today.
Shusaku: I see. The past and the paths we did not choose, I guess, are really like a dream, if you think about it. Suzu, choosing to marry you was the best decision of my life.

1. 下線部(1)が「彼が忘れたノートを持って」という意味になるように, (   )内の語句を適切に並べかえなさい。【表現と文法の知識】 (3点)

2. 空所(2)に入る最も適当な語を選びなさい。【語彙の知識】 (2点)
   ア. From   イ. In   ウ. On   エ. To

3. 下線部(3)のhave a chatに最も近い意味を表す語を, 本文中から1語で抜き出しなさい。
   (   )   【語彙と表現の知識】 (3点)

4. 下線部(4), (5)の語を適切な形に変えなさい。【表現と文法の知識】 (各2点)
   (4)
   (5)

5. 次の問いに英語で答えなさい。【内容についての思考力・判断力・表現力】 (各4点)
   (1) What did Shusaku actually want to do when he asked Suzu to come to his office?

   (2) What was Shusaku's best decision?

A Translate the English into Japanese and the Japanese into English. 【語彙の知識】(各1点)

1. gradually 副 A2 　[　　　　　]　2. ＿＿＿＿＿ 名 B1　姪

3. raid 名 　[　　　　　]　4. ＿＿＿＿＿ 形　爆発していない

5. explode 動 B2 　[　　　　　]　6. ＿＿＿＿＿ 形 A2　病気の

B Choose the word whose underlined part is pronounced differently from the other three. 【発音の知識】　　　　　(各2点)

1. ア. h<u>ar</u>d　　　イ. sm<u>ar</u>tphone　ウ. st<u>ar</u>t　　　エ. w<u>ar</u>

2. ア. bom<u>b</u>　　　イ. jo<u>b</u>　　　　ウ. mem<u>b</u>er　　エ. note<u>b</u>ook

3. ア. expl<u>o</u>de　イ. sh<u>ou</u>lder　　ウ. s<u>o</u>cial　　エ. thr<u>ou</u>gh

C Complete the following English sentences to match the Japanese. 【表現と文法の知識】

(各3点)

1. 子供のころに手をつないで父と歩いたのを覚えています。

I remember that I walked with my father (　　　　　) (　　　　　)

(　　　　　) in my childhood.

2. あなたのコンピュータのどこが悪いのかわかりましたか。

Have you (　　　　　) out (　　　　　) is wrong with your computer?

3. 上司に対するみんなの印象はあなたと同じものです。

Everyone's impression of our boss is (　　　　　) (　　　　　)

(　　　　　) yours.

D Arrange the words in the proper order to match the Japanese. 【表現と文法の知識・技能】

(各3点)

1. 手術の後，彼女の状態はよくなっています。

(better / condition / getting / her / is) after the operation.

＿＿＿＿＿＿＿＿＿＿＿＿＿＿＿＿＿＿＿＿＿＿＿＿＿＿＿＿＿

2. ヴィヴィアンは教科書を忘れたので，私と教科書を共有しました。

I (my / shared / textbook / Vivian / with) because she forgot hers.

＿＿＿＿＿＿＿＿＿＿＿＿＿＿＿＿＿＿＿＿＿＿＿＿＿＿＿＿＿

3. 彼がそのスマートフォンをいつ買ったのかは知りません。

I don't (bought / he / know / the smartphone / when).

＿＿＿＿＿＿＿＿＿＿＿＿＿＿＿＿＿＿＿＿＿＿＿＿＿＿＿＿＿

Read the following passage and answer the questions below.

Gradually, the situation gets worse. Suzu and her niece experience an air raid. When they are walking hand in hand after the raid, an unexploded bomb explodes. Her niece (1)(kill) and Suzu loses her right hand.

About four months after the war ends, Suzu finds "the new bomb" has taken the lives of her mother and father. Her younger sister is ill in bed. (2)She (lost / people / she / loves / has).

Through the movie, (3)we can find out how people lived during the war. They led ordinary lives. They shared time (4) their families. Sometimes they laughed together, and sometimes they cried together. Our lives today are the same as (5)theirs were. The movie shows that such ordinary lives are really precious.

1. 下線部(1)の語を適切な形に変えなさい。【文法の知識】 (2点)

2. 下線部(2)を「彼女は愛する人たちを失った。」という意味になるように, ( )内の語を適切に並べかえなさい。【表現と文法の知識】 (3点)

3. 下線部(3)を日本語にしなさい。【表現と文法の知識】 (3点)

4. 空所(4)に入る最も適当な前置詞を答えなさい。【表現の知識】 (2点)

( )

5. 下線部(5)を英語2語で言いかえたとき, ( )に入る最も適当な語を答えなさい。

their ( ) 【内容についての思考力・判断力・表現力】 (2点)

6. 次の問いに英語で答えなさい。【内容についての思考力・判断力・表現力】 (各4点)

(1) What happened to Suzu when an unexploded bomb exploded?

(2) According to the movie, what is really precious?

Should Stores Stay Open for 24 Hours? Part 1

/50

A Translate the English into Japanese and the Japanese into English.【語彙の知識】(各1点)

1. grant 動 B1   [   ]   2. .... 名 A2   長所，メリット

3. .... 形 A2   便利な   4. bill 名 A2   [   ]

5. analyst 名 B2   [   ]   6. .... 副 A2   特に，とりわけ

B Choose the word which has primary stress on a different syllable from the other three.【アクセントの知識】   (各2点)

1. ア. busi-ness   イ. mod-el   ウ. pack-age   エ. po-lice

2. ア. ad-van-tage   イ. an-a-lyst   ウ. con-ven-ience   エ. pro-duc-tion

3. ア. cer-e-mo-ny   イ. es-pe-cial-ly   ウ. in-ter-est-ing   エ. or-di-nar-y

C Complete the following English sentences to match the Japanese.【表現の知識】 (各3点)

1. 兄が手伝ってくれたおかげで宿題が終わった。

   (   ) (   ) my brother's help, I finished my homework.

2. 野生動物がこの道路を渡るとき，その命がしばしば危険にさらされている。

   Wild animals' lives are often (   ) (   ) when they cross this road.

3. やるべき仕事が多すぎたので，私は助けを求めた。

   I (   ) (   ) help because I had too much work to do.

D Arrange the words in the proper order to match the Japanese.【表現と文法の知識・技能】

(各3点)

1. 医者は私にしばらくベッドで横になっていなければならないと言った。

   The doctor (had / I / me / told / that / to) stay in bed for a while.

   ....

2. 叔父は私たちによい知らせを届けてくれた。

   My uncle (brought / good / news / some / us).

   ....

3. 私は当然夫もいっしょに福岡に来てくれると思っている。

   I (for / granted / it / my husband / take / that) will come to Fukuoka with me.

   ....

E Read the following passage and answer the questions below.

There are a lot of stores and restaurants around us. We take (1)it for granted that some of them are open for 24 hours. This business model has been popular. It (2) us some advantages.

(3), our lives have become convenient. At a convenience store, we can buy things, pay bills, and mail packages at any time. People who work late at night can eat at a 24-hour restaurant before or after work.

Second, our lives have become safer thanks to 24-hour stores and restaurants. (4)(ask / can / for / help / in danger / people) there. Analysts (5) us that convenience stores play the role of *koban*, or police boxes, especially at night.

1. 下線部(1)は何を指していますか。日本語で答えなさい。【表現と文法の知識】　　　　(3点)

　　　　　　　　　　　　　　　　　　　　　　　　　　　　　　　　　　　　　

2. 空所(2)に入る最も適当な語(句)を選びなさい。【文法の知識】　　　　　　　　(2点)
　　ア. has been brought　　　　　　　イ. has brought
　　ウ. is brought　　　　　　　　　　エ. was brought

3. 空所(3)に入る最も適当な語(句)を選びなさい。【文法の知識】　　　　　　　　(2点)
　　ア. At first　　　　イ. At first sight　　ウ. First　　　　エ. For the first time

4. 下線部(4)の(　　)内の語句を適切に並べかえなさい。【表現と文法の知識】　　　(3点)

　　　　　　　　　　　　　　　　　　　　　　　　　　　　　　　　　　　　　

5. 空所(5)に入る最も適当な語を選びなさい。【語彙の知識】　　　　　　　　　　(2点)
　　ア. say　　　　　　イ. speak　　　　　ウ. talk　　　　　エ. tell

6. 次の問いに英語で答えなさい。【内容についての思考力・判断力・表現力】　　　　(各4点)
　　(1) Thanks to 24-hour restaurants, what can people who work late at night do?

　　　　　　　　　　　　　　　　　　　　　　　　　　　　　　　　　　　　　

　　(2) What role do convenience stores play especially at night?

Should Stores Stay Open for 24 Hours? Part 2

/50

A Translate the English into Japanese and the Japanese into English.【語彙の知識】(各1点)

1. necessity 名 B2 [　　　　　] 　2. _____ 前 B2 …と違って

3. economy 名 B1 [　　　　　] 　4. rapidly 副 B1 [　　　　　]

5. _____ 名 B1 需要，必要性 　6. _____ 動 A2 …を許す，…を認める

B Choose the word whose underlined part is pronounced differently from the other three.【発音の知識】

(各2点)

1. ア. da<u>n</u>ger 　イ. dema<u>n</u>d 　ウ. gra<u>n</u>t 　エ. ra<u>p</u>idly

2. ア. all<u>ow</u> 　イ. b<u>o</u>th 　ウ. <u>o</u>nly 　エ. <u>o</u>pen

3. ア. b<u>i</u>ll 　イ. b<u>u</u>siness 　ウ. <u>u</u>nlike 　エ. w<u>o</u>men

C Complete the following English sentences to match the Japanese.【表現の知識】(各3点)

1. 通常の授業とは違って，オンライン授業はよく眠くなる。

(　　　　　　　) normal classes, online classes often make me sleepy.

2. 私は当時一人暮らしをしていた。

I was living alone (　　　　　) that (　　　　　).

3. この学校は1960年代後半に建てられた。

This school was built in (　　　　　) (　　　　　) 1960s.

D Arrange the words in the proper order to match the Japanese.【表現と文法の知識・技能】

(各3点)

1. 人々が在宅で働くことが社会的に求められている。

There is (a / demand / for / people / social / to) work at home.

_____

2. 鍵をかけていないと，自転車は簡単に持って行かれてしまいます。

If you don't lock your bicycle, (away / be / can / it / taken) easily.

_____

3. 両親は私が夜遅くまで外にいることを許してくれなかった。

My parents (allow / didn't / me / stay / to) out until late at night.

_____

E Read the following passage and answer the questions below.

Convenience stores started (1) an ice shop in the U.S. in the 1920s. Later, the ice shop started to sell daily necessities and food as well. In the 1970s, this idea came to Japan. (2) convenience stores now, stores at that time were only open from early in the morning till late at night.

Until the 1970s, (3)(almost / no stores / open / or restaurants / there / were) at night in Japan. Many Japanese people at that time worked during the day and stayed home at night.

<A> The Japanese economy developed rapidly, especially in the early 1970s. <B> The change in people's working styles allowed around-the-clock stores to appear in Japan. <C> Now, 24-hour convenience stores can (4)(see) everywhere. <D>

1. 空所(1), (2)に入る最も適当な語を選びなさい。【語彙と表現の知識】　　　　(各2点)

   (1) ア. for　　　　　イ. in　　　　　ウ. on　　　　　エ. with

   (2) ア. As　　　　　イ. Like　　　　ウ. Unlike　　　エ. With

2. 下線部(3)が「夜間に開いている店やレストランはほとんどなかった」という意味になるように, (　　)内の語句を適切に並べかえなさい。【表現と文法の知識】　　　　(3点)

3. 下線部(4)の語を適切な形に変えなさい。【文法の知識】　　　　(2点)

4. 本文中の<A>～<D>のうち, 下の英文を入れるのに最も適当な箇所を選びなさい。

【内容についての思考力・判断力・表現力】 (3点)

There was social demand for people to work at night.

   (　　　　　　　)

5. 次の問いに英語で答えなさい。【内容についての思考力・判断力・表現力】　　　　(各4点)

   (1) When did the idea of convenience stores come to Japan?

   (2) What allowed around-the-clock stores to appear in Japan?

A Translate the English into Japanese and the Japanese into English.【語彙の知識】(各1点)

1. .... 名 A2　短所, デメリット　　2. contribute 動 B1　[　　　　　　　　]

3. .... 動 B1　…を必要とする　　4. .... 名 B1　不足

5. population 名 A2　　[　　　　　　　]　　6. .... 動 B1　減少する

B Choose the word which has primary stress on a different syllable from the other three.【アクセントの知識】　(各2点)

1. ア. de-mand　　　イ. e-mit　　　ウ. em-ploy　　　エ. short-age

2. ア. con-trib-ute　　イ. de-vel-op　　ウ. en-er-gy　　エ. ex-am-ple

3. ア. e-con-o-my　　イ. ne-ces-si-ty　　ウ. pop-u-la-tion　　エ. so-ci-e-ty

C Complete the following English sentences to match the Japanese.【表現の知識】　(各3点)

1. 運転中のスマホの使用がこの交通事故の一因であった。

Smartphone use while driving (　　　　　　　) (　　　　　　　) this traffic accident.

2. その箱はいらないから捨てていいよ。

I don't need that box, so you can (　　　　　　　) it (　　　　　　　).

3. テニスの試合は大雨のせいで中止になった。

The tennis match was canceled (　　　　　　　) (　　　　　　　) heavy rain.

D Arrange the words in the proper order to match the Japanese.【表現と文法の知識・技能】

(各3点)

1. あなたに必要なのはゆっくり眠ることだ。

(is / need / sleep / to / what / you) well.

2. たしかに彼は英語が苦手だが, 数学の能力はすばらしいものがある。

(he / is / is / it / that / true) not good at English, but his math skills are excellent.

3. 生徒たちは先生の話を聞くために話をやめた。

The students (listen / stopped / talking / to / to) the teacher.

E Read the following passage and answer the questions below.

It is true that 24-hour stores have some advantages, (1) they also have disadvantages. For example, (2)they contribute to environmental problems. (3)(for / opening / requires / stores / 24 hours) a lot of energy and emits CO_2. In addition, stores throw away much unsold food.

A labor shortage is another problem. Due to the falling birthrate and aging population, the number of people (4) can work late at night has been decreasing. Owners of convenience stores think that it is difficult to employ enough staff members.

Should stores stay open for 24 hours? It is (5)(about / our society / think / to / time / what) really needs. Some stores have stopped (6)(open) for 24 hours. Time will tell.

1. 空所(1), (4)に入る最も適当な語を選びなさい。【文法の知識, 内容についての思考力・判断力・表現力】

(各1点)

(1) ア. and　　　イ. but　　　ウ. or　　　エ. so
(4) ア. what　　　イ. which　　　ウ. who　　　エ. whom

2. 下線部(2)は何を指していますか。日本語で答えなさい。【内容についての思考力・判断力・表現力】 (2点)

_____

3. 下線部(3), (5)の（　　　）内の語句を適切に並べかえなさい。【表現と文法の知識】　　(各3点)

(3) _____

(5) _____

4. 下線部(6)の語を適切な形に変えなさい。【文法の知識】 (2点)

_____

5. 次の問いに英語で答えなさい。【内容についての思考力・判断力・表現力】 (各4点)

(1) What do 24-hour stores throw away?

_____

(2) What causes a labor shortage in 24-hour stores?

_____

Lesson 7 — Should Stores Stay Open for 24 Hours? Part 4

/50

A Translate the English into Japanese and the Japanese into English. 【語彙の知識】（各1点）

1. _____ 形 B1　不可欠の，必須の　　2. _____ 動 A2　…だろうかと思う

3. _____ 名 A2　犯罪　　　　　　　　4. _____ 名 A2　生活様式

5. self-service 形 B1　[　　　　　　　]　　6. common 形 A2　[　　　　　　　]

B Choose the word whose underlined part is pronounced differently from the other three. 【発音の知識】　　　　　　　　　　　　　　　　　　　　（各2点）

1. ア. bec<u>o</u>me　　イ. c<u>o</u>mmon　　ウ. ec<u>o</u>nomy　　エ. m<u>o</u>dern

2. ア. conv<u>e</u>nience　　イ. decr<u>ea</u>se　　ウ. <u>e</u>ssential　　エ. m<u>ea</u>n

3. ア. cr<u>i</u>me　　イ. l<u>i</u>festyle　　ウ. pol<u>i</u>ce　　エ. soc<u>i</u>ety

C Complete the following English sentences to match the Japanese. 【表現と文法の知識】

（各3点）

1. 彼は前日に2つのテストがあったのでとても疲れていた。

He was very tired because he (　　　　　　) (　　　　　　) two tests the day before.

2. 次の授業にはこの教科書が必要不可欠ですよ。

This textbook (　　　　　) (　　　　　) (　　　　　) the next class.

3. 来週東京に行くそうですね。

(　　　　　) (　　　　　　) you are going to Tokyo next week.

D Arrange the words in the proper order to match the Japanese. 【表現と文法の知識・技能】

（各3点）

1. 彼らはだれだろう。見たことのない人たちだよ。

(are / I / they / who / wonder). I've never seen them.

_____

2. 家に着いたときには母は出かけてしまっていた。

My mother (gone out / got / had / home / I / when).

_____

3. 彼の考え方を変えるのは難しい。

It is (change / difficult / his way / of / thinking / to).

_____

E Read the following passage and answer the questions below.

David: Do you think (1)(for / open / should / stay / stores) 24 hours?

Taro: Yes. They're essential for us in modern society. I (2)(had / how / lived / people / wonder) before convenience stores started. Thanks to 24-hour stores, we can buy things at night.

David: I see. You mean our lives have become convenient. How about you, Kumi?

Kumi: I don't think stores should stay open for 24 hours. (3)(Go) shopping late at night can be dangerous. There are a lot of crimes, especially at night. I really think we have to find new lifestyles without 24-hour stores.

David: That's interesting. (4), right? In Europe, most stores are (5)(close) at night. I hear that self-service stores will become more common in Japan.

1. 下線部(1)，(2)の( )内の語を適切に並べかえなさい。【表現と文法の知識】　　　　　（各3点）

    (1) _____

    (2) _____

2. 下線部(3)，(5)の語を適切な形に変えなさい。【語彙と文法の知識】　　　　　（各2点）

    (3) _____

    (5) _____

3. 空所(4)に入る最も適当な表現を選びなさい。【内容についての思考力・判断力・表現力】　　　　　（2点）

    ア．We should not go shopping alone

    イ．We have to decrease the number of crimes first

    ウ．We have to change our way of thinking

    エ．We should have more convenience stores for safety

4. 次の問いに英語で答えなさい。【内容についての思考力・判断力・表現力】　　　　　（各4点）

    (1) Why does Taro think 24-hour stores are essential?

    _____

    (2) What are stores in Europe like?

    _____

Our Future with Artificial Intelligence Part 1

/50

A Translate the English into Japanese and the Japanese into English. 【語彙の知識】（各1点）

1. attitude 名 A2 [   ]   2. issue 名 A2 [   ]

3. _____ 形 A2 消極的な, 後ろ向きの   4. concerning 前 B2 [   ]

5. _____ 名 A2 影響   6. _____ 名 A2 イメージ, 印象

B Choose the word which has primary stress on a different syllable from the other three. 【アクセントの知識】

（各2点）

1. ア. are-a   イ. con-cern   ウ. im-age   エ. im-pact

2. ア. at-ti-tude   イ. con-sid-er   ウ. im-por-tant   エ. un-eas-y

3. ア. dan-ger-ous   イ. per-cent-age   ウ. pop-u-lar   エ. pos-i-tive

C Complete the following English sentences to match the Japanese. 【表現と文法の知識】

（各3点）

1. あなたの考えが正しいと思う人もいるが, そう思わない人もいるかもしれない。

（   ） people think your idea is right, but （   ） may not think so.

2. その歌手は20代の女性に特に人気がある。

The singer is especially popular among women （   ） their （   ）.

3. トムは働き者だ。一方で, ケンはなまけ者だ。

Tom is hardworking. （   ） the other （   ）, Ken is lazy.

D Arrange the words in the proper order to match the Japanese. 【表現と文法の知識・技能】

（各3点）

1. テレビ番組は子供に強い影響を及ぼす。

TV programs (a / children / have / impact / on / strong).

_____

2. 向こうで犬と歩いているあの男の子を知っています。

I know (is / that / the boy / walking / with) a dog over there.

_____

3. 最近の調査によると, 車を運転する人の数は増えています。

A recent research (drivers / of / shows / that / the number) is increasing.

_____

E Read the following passage and answer the questions below.

AI (1)has been an important issue for us. (2) people talk about the bright future that AI will bring us. (3) worry that AI may take away our jobs. Let's look at the figures below, and consider these differences in attitudes toward AI.

Figure 1 shows that 41.8% of people in their twenties worry about losing their jobs due to AI. (4)On the other hand, only 19.9% of people aged over 60 worry about it. Younger people feel more uneasy about this negative side of AI.

(5) other areas of AI, Figure 2 shows that younger people have more positive attitudes toward AI. About 10% of people in their twenties and thirties think AI will have a favorable impact on their lives. About half this percentage of older people have positive images of AI.

1. 下線部(1)の現在完了と同じ用法を含むものを選びなさい。【文法の知識】　　　(2点)
　　ア．I have already eaten lunch.　　　イ．I have been to Nagoya once.
　　ウ．I have finished my homework.　　エ．I have known him for twenty years.

2. 空所(2)，(3)に入る最も適当な語(句)をそれぞれ選びなさい。【表現の知識】　　(各2点)
　　ア．Other　　　　イ．Others　　　　ウ．Some　　　　エ．The others
　　(2) (　　　　) 　(3) (　　　　)

3. 下線部(4)の文の主語と(述語)動詞を答えなさい。【表現と文法の知識】　　　(各2点)
　　主語：
　　(述語)動詞：

4. 空所(5)に入る最も適当な語を選びなさい。【語彙の知識】　　　(2点)
　　ア．Concerning　　　イ．Considering　　ウ．During　　　エ．Including

5. 次の問いに英語で答えなさい。【内容についての思考力・判断力・表現力】　　(各4点)
　　(1) What do about half of the people in their twenties worry about?

　　(2) What percent of older people think about AI positively?

A Translate the English into Japanese and the Japanese into English.【語彙の知識】(各1点)

1. accuracy 名 B1   [   ]   2. .... 動 B1   …を可能にする

3. feature 名 A2   [   ]   4. .... 動 B1   …を認識する

5. intersection 名 B2   [   ]   6. .... 前 A2   …の内側に, …の中に

B Choose the word whose underlined part is pronounced differently from the other three.【発音の知識】(各2点)

1. ア. feature   イ. instead   ウ. repeat   エ. uneasy

2. ア. contribute   イ. driving   ウ. precisely   エ. recognize

3. ア. accuracy   イ. image   ウ. task   エ. traffic

C Complete the following English sentences to match the Japanese.【表現と文法の知識】(各3点)

1. 妹は一人でカレーが作れます。

   My sister can cook curry and rice (   ) (   ).

2. 私はジャズを聴きながら車で仕事に行くことが多い。

   I often drive to work, (   ) to jazz.

3. 子供にとって善悪の区別をすることは簡単ではない。

   It is not easy for children to (   ) right (   ) wrong.

D Arrange the words in the proper order to match the Japanese.【表現と文法の知識・技能】(各3点)

1. これはあなたが探しているペンではないですか。

   Is this (are / for / looking / the pen / which / you)?

2. インターネットのおかげで人々は簡単にお互いにコミュニケーションをとることができる。

   The Internet (easily communicate / enables / with / people / to) each other.

3. この薬は1日に3回飲まなければいけません。

   This medicine (be / should / three / taken / times) a day.

E Read the following passage and answer the questions below.

We often talk about AI, but what is it exactly? It is (1)(a computer program / a lot of / can / do / tasks / which) with accuracy. It repeats the tasks, (2)(keep) its accuracy over a long time. Even human-level AI can be realized by deep learning.

Deep learning is a technology which enables a machine to learn by itself, like humans do. This type of AI discovers different features in an object and repeats the process until it can recognize the object. As a result, it can learn to tell an object (3) others with accuracy.

(4)This technology is used for self-driving cars. The AI recognizes stop signs and traffic lights, so the self-driving cars stop precisely at intersections. Traffic lane lines are (5)(recognize), so cars keep within their own lanes. AI contributes to safe driving.

1. 下線部(1)の(　　)内の語句を適切に並べかえなさい。【表現と文法の知識】　　　　(3点)

　　．．

2. 下線部(2), (5)の語を適切な形に変えなさい。【文法の知識】　　　　(各2点)

　　(2) ．．

　　(5) ．．

3. 空所(3)に入る最も適当な語を選びなさい。【表現の知識】　　　　(2点)

　　ア. by　　　　　　　イ. for　　　　　　　ウ. from　　　　　　　エ. in

4. 下線部(4)は具体的には何を指していますか。英語2語で答えなさい。

【内容についての思考力・判断力・表現力】　(3点)

　　(　　　　　　　)(　　　　　　　)

5. 次の問いに英語で答えなさい。【内容についての思考力・判断力・表現力】　　　　(各4点)

　　(1) What is deep learning?

　　．．

　　．．

　　(2) Why can the self-driving cars stop precisely at intersections?

　　．．

Our Future with Artificial Intelligence Part 3

/50

A Translate the English into Japanese and the Japanese into English.【語彙の知識】(各1点)

1. .... 形 顔の
2. recognition 名 B2 [   ]
3. passenger 名 A2 [   ]
4. .... 動 A2 …を予測する
5. .... 形 A2 ありそうな, 起こりそうな
6. prevent 動 A2 [   ]

B Choose the word which has primary stress on a different syllable from the other three.【アクセントの知識】 (各2点)

1. ア. like-ly　　　イ. po-lice　　　ウ. pre-dict　　　エ. pre-vent
2. ア. ex-am-ple　　イ. how-ev-er　　ウ. pas-sen-ger　　エ. pre-cise-ly
3. ア. in-ter-sec-tion　イ. rec-og-ni-tion　ウ. sit-u-a-tion　エ. tech-nol-o-gy

C Complete the following English sentences to match the Japanese.【表現と文法の知識】

(各3点)

1. ここで働きたければ, 面接を受ける必要があります。

   If you want to work here, you (   ) (   ) have an interview.
2. 今夜は雪が降りそうだ。

   It's (   ) (   ) snow this evening.
3. 時がたつにつれて, 人々はその災害のことを忘れてしまった。

   (   ) time passed, people (   ) about the disaster.

D Arrange the words in the proper order to match the Japanese.【表現と文法の知識・技能】

(各3点)

1. 新薬のおかげでその病気が世界中に広がるのを防ぐことができた。

   (from / prevented / spreading / the disease / the new medicine) all over the world.

   ....

2. あなたが東京を出発する時間を教えてくれませんか。

   Can you tell me (leave / the time / Tokyo / when / will / you)?

   ....

3. 財布をなくした場所を覚えていません。

   I don't remember (I / lost / my wallet / the place / where).

   ....

E Read the following passage and answer the questions below.

AI is used in facial recognition technology at airports. Passengers now often need to wait in lines and show their passports and boarding passes at gates. Thanks to this technology, however, they won't need to do (1)these things, and they can save travel time.

AI is also useful for (2)(predict) the times when crimes are likely to happen. It can predict the places where crimes will happen, too. By using this technology, (3)police officers can prevent crimes from happening. As the number of crimes decreases, society will become safer.

AI, however, has some negative features. For example, it is becoming difficult for even AI engineers to understand AI's way of thinking exactly. (4)(Consider) the negative features, (5)(AI / must / to / try / use / we) carefully.

1. 下線部(1)は具体的には何を指していますか。日本語で答えなさい。

【内容についての思考力・判断力・表現力】 （3点）

2. 下線部(2)，(4)の語を適切な形に変えなさい。【文法の知識】　　　　　　（各2点）

(2)

(4)

3. 下線部(3)を日本語にしなさい。【表現と文法の知識】　　　　　　　　　　（2点）

4. 下線部(5)が「私たちはAIを慎重に使おうとしなければならない」という意味になるように、
（　　）内の語を適切に並べかえなさい。【表現と文法の知識】　　　　　　（3点）

5. 次の問いに英語で答えなさい。【内容についての思考力・判断力・表現力】　（各4点）

(1) If AI is used at airports, can we save travel time?

(2) What will happen to society as the number of crimes decreases?

Our Future with Artificial Intelligence Part 4

/50

A Translate the English into Japanese and the Japanese into English.【語彙の知識】(各1点)

1. _____ 形 A2　医療の
2. citizen 名 A2　[　　　　　　　]
3. relieve 動 B2　[　　　　　　]
4. _____ 名 B1　負担, 重荷
5. emergency 形　[　　　　　　]
6. _____ 名 A2　質

B Choose the word whose underlined part is pronounced differently from the other three.【発音の知識】(各2点)

1. ア. c<u>o</u>pe　　　イ. l<u>o</u>cal　　　ウ. <u>o</u>fficer　　　エ. smartph<u>o</u>ne
2. ア. an<u>o</u>ther　　イ. c<u>o</u>mputer　　ウ. g<u>o</u>vernment　　エ. s<u>u</u>ddenly
3. ア. emer<u>g</u>ency　イ. ener<u>g</u>y　　ウ. percenta<u>g</u>e　　エ. reco<u>g</u>nition

C Complete the following English sentences to match the Japanese.【表現と文法の知識】
(各3点)

1. 昨日はとても暑い日だったので, たくさんの生徒が次々と体調を崩しました。

　 Since it was a very hot day yesterday, many students felt sick (　　　　　　)
　 after (　　　　　　).

2. あなたの考え方は私とまるで違います。

　 (　　　　　　) (　　　　　　) you think is totally different from mine.

3. あなたはこの状況に対処できますか。

　 Can you (　　　　　　) (　　　　　　) this situation?

D Arrange the words in the proper order to match the Japanese.【表現と文法の知識・技能】
(各3点)

1. 先生が怒った理由が私にはわかりません。

　 I don't know (angry / got / the reason / the teacher / why).

2. そのホテルは宿泊客に最高のサービスを提供してくれる。

　 (guests / offers / service / the best / the hotel / to).

3. この機会を有意義に活用してください。

　 (good / make / of / please / use) this opportunity.

E Read the following passage and answer the questions below.

Local governments are trying to use AI to offer better medical services to their citizens. When a small child suddenly gets sick, young parents often feel uneasy. (1)There is now an AI system (can / give / helpful advice / that / to / uneasy parents). The way they use the system is by entering medical information (2) their computers or smartphones.

The AI system also helps to relieve the burdens of people working in emergency medical services. Emergency calls come one (3) another, especially (3) local clinics are closed. The AI system can try to cope with emergency cases before workers (4)do.

AI will be used in more fields, and it will improve our quality of life. We will be able to live well with AI if we (5) make good use of it.

1. 下線部(1)が「今では，不安な親に有益なアドバイスを提供することができるAIシステムがある。」という意味になるように，(　　)内の語句を適切に並べかえなさい。【表現と文法の知識】 （3点）

2. 空所(2)，(5)に入る最も適当な語を選びなさい。【表現と文法の知識】 （各2点）

(2) ア. at　　　　イ. for　　　　ウ. from　　　　エ. into
(5) ア. can　　　イ. may　　　　ウ. must　　　　エ. will

3. 空所(3)に共通して入る最も適当な語を答えなさい。【語彙と表現の知識】 （2点）
(　　　　　　　　)

4. 下線部(4)は具体的には何を指していますか。英語4語で答えなさい。【表現と文法の知識】 （3点）

5. 次の問いに英語で答えなさい。【内容についての思考力・判断力・表現力】 （各4点）
(1) How do young parents feel when their small child suddenly gets sick?

(2) What will AI improve when it is used in more fields?

Stop Microplastic Pollution! Part 1

/50

A Translate the English into Japanese and the Japanese into English.【語彙の知識】(各1点)

1. _____ 形　氷で冷やした
2. counter 名 B2　[　　　　　]
3. _____ 名 B1　ストロー
4. globally 副 B2　[　　　　　]
5. _____ 名　マイクロプラスチック
6. _____ 形 B1　深刻な

B Choose the word which has primary stress on a different syllable from the other three.【アクセントの知識】(各2点)

1. ア. dis-cuss　　イ. plas-tic　　ウ. prod-uct　　エ. re-cent
2. ア. In-ter-net　　イ. re-al-ly　　ウ. se-ri-ous　　エ. to-geth-er
3. ア. dif-fer-ent　　イ. glob-al-ly　　ウ. gov-ern-ment　　エ. pol-lu-tion

C Complete the following English sentences to match the Japanese.【表現と文法の知識】(各3点)

1. 私は今日いつものように朝7時に家を出ました。

I left home at 7:00 a.m. (　　　　　) (　　　　　) today.

2. 弟はリビングの掃除を手伝いました。

My brother (　　　　　) (　　　　　) clean the living room.

3. 彼女は秋に入学できる大学を探しています。

She is (　　　　　) (　　　　　) a college she can enter in the fall.

D Arrange the words in the proper order to match the Japanese.【表現と文法の知識・技能】(各3点)

1. 父は健康のためにお酒を飲むのをやめました。

(for / his health / my father / drinking / stopped).

_____

2. コーチは私たちに相手チームのビデオを見させます。

(a video / makes / the coach / watch / us) of the opposing team.

_____

3. その問題については私はまったくわかりません。ケイトに聞いてみましょう。

I (about / have / idea / no / the problem). Let's ask Kate.

_____

E Read the following passage and answer the questions below.

Manabu   2 hours ago
  This afternoon, I went to a café with Takashi. I ordered some iced coffee as
usual, but something was different today. The person at the counter didn't give
me a plastic straw. She said, "We have stopped serving plastic straws globally.
We want to (1)(from / help / save / the environment / to) microplastic pollution."
What are microplastics? I searched (2) information about the microplastic
problem on the Internet, and I learned that it is becoming very serious. I was
(3)(shock). The government in every country should make its people (4)
plastic products.
  Now, I really want to do something to solve this problem. Let's discuss the
problem together.
Takashi   30 minutes ago
  We use a lot of plastics every day. Should we stop using them?
Vivian   45 minutes ago
  What can we do about this?
Kumi   1 hour ago
  I had no idea about this problem.

1. 下線部(1)の(　　)内の語句を適切に並べかえなさい。【表現の知識】　　　　　　　(3点)

　　　　　　　　　　　　　　　　　　　　　　　　　　　　　　　　　　　

2. 空所(2)に入る最も適当な語を選びなさい。【表現の知識】　　　　　　　　　　(3点)
　　ア. for　　　　　　　イ. in　　　　　　ウ. of　　　　　　エ. with

3. 下線部(3)の語を適切な形に変えなさい。【語彙と表現の知識】　　　　　　　　(3点)

　　　　　　　　　　　　　　　　　　　　　

4. 空所(4)に入る最も適当な語句を選びなさい。【表現と文法の知識】　　　　　　(3点)
　　ア. stop to waste　　イ. stop wasting　　ウ. to stop to waste エ. to stop wasting

5. 次の問いに英語で答えなさい。【内容についての思考力・判断力・表現力】　　　(各4点)
　(1) What does Manabu usually get when he orders some iced coffee at a café?

　　　　　　　　　　　　　　　　　　　　　　　　　　　　　　　　　　　

　(2) What did Manabu learn about microplastic problem on the Internet?

Stop Microplastic Pollution!

Part 2

/50

A Translate the English into Japanese and the Japanese into English. 【語彙の知識】(各1点)

1. .... 名 B1 砂
2. .... 名 B2 ミリメートル
3. diameter 名 B1 [   ]
4. expose 動 B1 [   ]
5. microbe 名 B2 [   ]
6. .... 動 A2 とどまる, 残る

B Choose the word whose underlined part is pronounced differently from the other three. 【発音の知識】 (各2点)

1. ア. b<u>ea</u>ch   イ. m<u>ea</u>n   ウ. m<u>i</u>cro   エ. p<u>ie</u>ce
2. ア. exp<u>o</u>se   イ. micr<u>o</u>be   ウ. sm<u>a</u>ll   エ. thr<u>ow</u>
3. ア. bec<u>o</u>me   イ. d<u>i</u>ameter   ウ. res<u>u</u>lt   エ. s<u>u</u>nlight

C Complete the following English sentences to match the Japanese. 【表現の知識】 (各3点)

1. 私が住んでいる町の人口は10万人以下です。

The town I live in has (   ) (   ) 100,000 people.

2. 私は長い間祖父母と会っていません。

I haven't seen my grandparents (   ) a long (   ).

3. この大学のほとんどの学生はコンピュータの操作に慣れています。

(   ) (   ) the students at this university are used to working with computers.

D Arrange the words in the proper order to match the Japanese. 【表現と文法の知識・技能】

(各3点)

1. 私は家の前で犬が私を待っているのを見ました。

I (for / me / my dog / saw / waiting) in front of my house.

_____

2. 彼らは壁の汚れを水で洗い流した。

They (down / on / the dirt / the wall / washed) with water.

_____

3. 私が昨夜会った女性は有名な学者です。

(I / is / last night / met / the woman) a famous scholar.

_____

E Read the following passage and answer the questions below.

When you walk along the beach, you may (1)(a lot of / objects / see / shining / small) in the sand. Perhaps they are "microplastics."

"Micro" means "very (2)." Microplastics are very small pieces of plastic garbage. They are less than about five millimeters in diameter. Plastics easily break into small pieces when they are heated or (3)(expose) to sunlight for a long time.

Wood pieces and grass on the beach can (4)(eat) by microbes, but plastics often remain there. Plastics may become smaller, but they do not disappear easily. (5) them may be washed down into the sea and stay there forever. As a result, the sea becomes the "dead end" of the plastics people throw away.

1. 下線部(1)の(　　)内の語句を適切に並べかえなさい。【表現と文法の知識】　　　　　　(3点)

2. 空所(2)に入る最も適当な語を，本文中から抜き出して答えなさい。【語彙の知識】　　　(2点)

(　　　　　　　　)

3. 下線部(3)，(4)の語を適切な形に変えなさい。【語彙の知識】　　　　　　　　　　　(各2点)

(3)

(4)

4. 空所(5)に入る最も適当な語(句)を選びなさい。【語彙と表現の知識】　　　　　　　　(3点)

ア. Almost　　　　　　イ. Almost of　　　　ウ. Most　　　　　　エ. Most of

5. 次の問いに英語で答えなさい。【内容についての思考力・判断力・表現力】　　　　　　(各4点)

(1) What is the diameter of microplastics?

(2) Where is the "dead end" of the plastics people throw away?

Stop Microplastic Pollution!

A Translate the English into Japanese and the Japanese into English. 【語彙の知識】(各1点)

1. .... 名 B1　海水　　　　　　　2. coast 名 A2　　　　　　[　　　　　　]

3. .... 動 A2　…を汚す　　　　　4. .... 名 A2　連鎖

5. shark 名　　　[　　　　　]　　　6. whale 名 B1　　　[　　　　　　]

B Choose the word whose underlined part is pronounced differently from the other three. 【発音の知識】　　　　　　　　　　　　　　　　　　　　　　(各2点)

1. ア. acc<u>o</u>rding　　イ. c<u>oa</u>st　　　ウ. <u>o</u>cean　　　エ. <u>o</u>ver

2. ア. <u>a</u>nimal　　　イ. f<u>a</u>ct　　　ウ. pl<u>a</u>nkton　　エ. t<u>o</u>n

3. ア. <u>e</u>very　　　イ. s<u>e</u>veral　　ウ. spr<u>ea</u>d　　エ. wh<u>a</u>le

C Complete the following English sentences to match the Japanese. 【表現と文法の知識】

(各3点)

1. 天気予報によれば，1週間晴天が続くそうだ。

(　　　　　　) (　　　　　　　　) the weather forecast, fine weather will continue

for a week.

2. 新幹線に乗れば，2時間で東京駅に着きます。

You will arrive at Tokyo Station in two hours, (　　　　　) you (　　　　　)

the *Shinkansen*.

3. 先生はときどき私と妹を間違えます。

Teachers sometimes (　　　　　) me (　　　　　) my younger sister.

D Arrange the words in the proper order to match the Japanese. 【表現と文法の知識・技能】

(各3点)

1. 私の弁当にはゆで卵が半分に切られて入っていました。

My *bento* (boiled / contained / cut / eggs / in half).

2. 私は学校から約5kmのところに住んでいる。

I live (about / away / five kilometers / from / the school).

3. 今年は地震などの自然災害が多かった。

We had (as / earthquakes / many / natural disasters / such) this year.

E Read the following passage and answer the questions below.

Microplastics are found in the oceans all over the world. According to a study, 2.4 pieces of microplastics were found in every ton of seawater, even at several kilometers away from the coast. Now, such (1)(pollute) seawater (2)(call) "plastic soup."

Microplastics spread through the food chain. Plankton are near the (3) of the food chain. The plankton may eat microplastics if they mistake (4)them for their food. Microplastic pollution spreads as small fish eat plankton and the bigger sea animals, such as sharks and whales, eat those small fish.

Such a situation may be bad for people's health because (5)(that / may / eat / have eaten / people / fish) microplastics. In fact, plastics are found within the fishes' bodies.

1. 下線部(1), (2)の語を適切な形に変えなさい。【文法の知識】　　　　　　　　(各2点)

    (1) _____

    (2) _____

2. 空所(3)に入る最も適当な語を選びなさい。【語彙と表現の知識】　　　　　　(2点)

    ア. bottom　　　　イ. middle　　　　ウ. top　　　　エ. upper

3. 下線部(4)は具体的には何を指していますか。最も適当な語を選びなさい。

                             【内容についての思考力・判断力・表現力】　(3点)

    ア. fish　　　　　　イ. microplastics　ウ. plankton　　　エ. seawater

4. 下線部(5)が「マイクロプラスチックを食べた魚を人が食べるかもしれない」という意味になるように, (　　)内の語句を適切に並べかえなさい。【表現と文法の知識】　　　　(3点)

_____

5. 次の問いに英語で答えなさい。【内容についての思考力・判断力・表現力】　　(各4点)

    (1) How many pieces of microplastics can be found in a ton of seawater?

_____

    (2) Where are plastics found in fish?

_____

Stop Microplastic Pollution!

Part 4

/50

A Translate the English into Japanese and the Japanese into English.【語彙の知識】(各1点)

1. _____ 名 A1 行動，活動　　2. _____ 動 A1 …を解決する

3. product 名 A2　　[　　　　　　] 　　4. submarine 形　　[　　　　　　]

5. situation 名 A2　　[　　　　　　] 　　6. _____ 形 A2 役に立つ

B Choose the word which has primary stress on a different syllable from the other three【アクセントの知識】 (各2点)

1. ア. a-round　　イ. fu-ture　　ウ. may-be　　エ. prob-lem

2. ア. a-mount　　イ. plas-tic　　ウ. prod-uct　　エ. use-ful

3. ア. ex-am-ple　　イ. for-ev-er　　ウ. how-ev-er　　エ. se-ri-ous

C Complete the following English sentences to match the Japanese.【表現と文法の知識】

(各3点)

1. 最近，ますます多くの学生が留学しています。

These days, (　　　　　) (　　　　　) (　　　　　) students are studying abroad.

2. 若者たちは被災地の人々を助けるために行動を起こしました。

Young people (　　　　　) (　　　　　) to help people in the disaster area.

3. もし私が彼女のメールアドレスを知っていたら，彼女にメールを送ることができるのに。

If I (　　　　　) her email address, I (　　　　　) send her an email.

D Arrange the words in the proper order to match the Japanese.【表現と文法の知識・技能】

(各3点)

1. たとえ今回失敗しても，私は自分の意志を変えません。

(even / fail / I / if / this / time), I will not change my will.

_____

2. 彼の講義はただ話が長いだけだったので，私は眠くなった。

As his lecture was just a long story, (made / it / sleepy / me).

_____

3. 何人かの生徒が野球部設立のために行動を開始した。

Some students (a baseball club / act / for / setting up / started / to).

_____

E Read the following passage and answer the questions below.

More and more countries have taken action to solve the microplastic problem. They have tried to (1)(cut / of / people / plastic / the amount / use). They hope that (2) plastic products will be used around the world.

Even young people can help to solve the problem. (3), an American girl made a submarine robot to find microplastics in the seawater. Such robots may help to clean the sea in the future.

Everybody can help to change the situation. You may say to yourself, "(4)Maybe if I ( ) a good idea, I ( ) ( ) something useful." However, even if you don't have a very good idea, you can say "no" to some plastic products and make the problem (5) serious. Let's act for a brighter future.

1. 下線部(1)の( )内の語句を適切に並べかえなさい。【表現の知識】　　　　　(3点)

2. 空所(2), (3), (5)に入る最も適当な語(句)を選びなさい。
【語彙と表現の知識, 内容についての思考力・判断力・表現力】 (各2点)

   (2) ア. fewer　　　　イ. less　　　　ウ. many　　　　エ. more

   (3) ア. As a result　イ. For example　ウ. However　　エ. In addition

   (5) ア. better　　　　イ. less　　　　ウ. more　　　　エ. much

3. 下線部(4)が「もしいいアイデアがあれば何か役に立つことができるかもしれないのに」という意味になるように, ( )に適語を補いなさい。【文法の知識】 (完答3点)

   Maybe if I (　　　　　　) a good idea, I (　　　　　) (　　　　　　) something useful

4. 次の問いに英語で答えなさい。【内容についての思考力・判断力・表現力】　　　　(各4点)

   (1) What did an American girl make?

   (2) Can all of us help to change the situation of the microplastic problem?

A Retrieved Reformation

Part 1

/50

A Translate the English into Japanese and the Japanese into English.【語彙の知識】(各 1 点)

1. release 動 B1　　　[　　　　　　　]　2. ＿＿＿＿＿＿＿ 名 B1　刑務所

3. ＿＿＿＿＿＿＿ 動 A2　…を盗む　　　4. detective 名 B1　　　[　　　　　　　]

5. ＿＿＿＿＿＿＿ 動 B1　…を逮捕する　　6. athletic 形 B1　　　[　　　　　　　]

B Choose the word whose underlined part is pronounced differently from the other three.【発音の知識】(各 2 点)

1. ア. l<u>o</u>wer　　　イ. <u>o</u>nly　　　ウ. st<u>o</u>len　　　エ. th<u>ou</u>ght

2. ア. <u>a</u>nother　　イ. b<u>a</u>nk　　　ウ. m<u>o</u>ney　　　エ. y<u>ou</u>ng

3. ア. after<u>noo</u>n　イ. f<u>u</u>ll　　　ウ. s<u>ui</u>tcase　　エ. thr<u>ou</u>gh

C Complete the following English sentences to match the Japanese.【表現の知識】(各 3 点)

1. 彼はテレビ番組で説得力のある意見を言うことで有名です。

He is (　　　　　　) (　　　　　　　　　) making convincing opinions on TV shows.

2. リビングには古い新聞でいっぱいの箱が置いてあった。

There are boxes (　　　　　　) (　　　　　　　) old newspapers in the living room.

3. 医者は診察のためにまず彼女の口の中をのぞき込んだ。

The doctor first (　　　　　　) (　　　　　　　) her mouth for an examination.

D Arrange the words in the proper order to match the Japanese.【表現と文法の知識・技能】

(各 3 点)

1. 私は窓を開けたままで外出してしまった。

I (open / out / the window / went / with).

_____

2. それがだれのバッグなのか知っていますか。

Do you (bag / is / it / know / whose)?

_____

3. 彼の理論はとても斬新なものだったので，だれも理解できなかった。

His theory (no / novel / one / so / that / was) could understand it.

_____

E Read the following passage and answer the questions below.

Jimmy Valentine was released from prison, and it was just a week later that a safe was broken open in Richmond, Indiana. Eight hundred dollars was stolen. Two weeks after that, a safe in Logansport was opened, and fifteen hundred dollars was taken. Everyone was shocked, as this safe was so strong that people thought no one could break it open. Then a safe in Jefferson City was opened, and five thousand dollars was stolen.

Ben Price was a detective. He was a big man, and famous for his skill at (1)(solve) very difficult and important cases. So now he began to work on these three cases. He was the only person who knew how Jimmy did his job. People (2)(full / money / of / safes / with) were glad to hear that Ben Price was at work trying to arrest Mr. Valentine.

One afternoon, Jimmy Valentine and his suitcase arrived in a small town (3)(name) Elmore. Jimmy, looking like an athletic young man just home from college, walked down the street toward the hotel.

A young lady walked across the street, passed him at the corner, and went through a door with a sign "The Elmore Bank" on it. Jimmy Valentine looked into her eyes, forgot (4) once what he was, and became another man. The young lady looked back at him, and then lowered her eyes as her face became (5). Handsome young men like Jimmy were not often seen in Elmore.

1. 下線部(1)，(3)の語を適切な形に変えなさい。【文法の知識】　　　　　　　(各3点)

   (1) _____　　　(3) _____

2. 下線部(2)の(　　)内の語を適切に並べかえなさい。【表現と文法の知識】　　　(3点)

   _____

3. 空所(4)，(5)に入る最も適当な語を選びなさい。【語彙の知識】　　　　　　(3点)

   (4) ア. at　　　　　イ. for　　　　　ウ. in　　　　　エ. on
   (5) ア. blue　　　　イ. dark　　　　ウ. pale　　　　エ. red

4. 次の問いに英語で答えなさい。【内容についての思考力・判断力・表現力】　　(各4点)

   (1) How much money did Jimmy steal after being released from prison?

   _____

   (2) What did Ben know about Jimmy?

   _____

A Retrieved Reformation

Part 2

/50

A Translate the English into Japanese and the Japanese into English.【語彙の知識】(各1点)

1. pretend 動 A2   [   ]   2. manner 名 A2   [   ]

3. ＿＿＿＿＿ 形 A2 心地よい, 感じのよい   4. identity 名 B1   [   ]

5. ＿＿＿＿＿ 名 A2 発作, 発病   6. ＿＿＿＿＿ 名 A2   結婚式

B Choose the word which has primary stress on a different syllable from the other three.【アクセントの知識】

(各2点)

1. ア. no-tice   イ. pleas-ant   ウ. pre-tend   エ. suit-case

2. ア. at-tack   イ. im-press   ウ. man-ner   エ. re-main

3. ア. com-mu-ni-ty   イ. i-den-ti-ty   ウ. im-por-tant-ly   エ. in-for-ma-tion

C Complete the following English sentences to match the Japanese.【表現と文法の知識】

(各3点)

1. 大学卒業後, トムとケイトはベンチャー企業を設立しました。

After graduating from university, Tom and Kate (   ) (   ) a venture company.

2. 明日の便の窓側の席を予約したいのですが。

I (   ) (   ) to reserve a window seat for tomorrow's flight.

3. 学は地域の歴史を調べることにしました。

Manabu decided to (   ) (   ) the local history.

D Arrange the words in the proper order to match the Japanese.【表現と文法の知識・技能】

(各3点)

1. 私は昨日, ジャックが学校の周りを走っているのを見ました。

I (around / Jack / running / saw / the school) yesterday.

＿＿＿＿＿＿＿＿＿＿＿＿＿＿＿＿＿＿＿＿＿＿＿＿＿＿＿

2. 先生は私たちに教室でスマートフォンを使わないように注意した。

The teacher (not / the smartphone / to / us / use / warned) in the classroom.

＿＿＿＿＿＿＿＿＿＿＿＿＿＿＿＿＿＿＿＿＿＿＿＿＿＿＿

3. 意見交換をしているうちに, 私たちはお互いの考えを理解するようになった。

After exchanging opinions, we (each / got / other's / thoughts / to / understand).

＿＿＿＿＿＿＿＿＿＿＿＿＿＿＿＿＿＿＿＿＿＿＿＿＿＿＿

E Read the following passage and answer the questions below.

Jimmy saw a boy playing on the steps of the bank and began asking him questions about the town. After a time, the young lady came out of the bank. This time she pretended not to notice the young man with the suitcase, and went her way. "Isn't that young lady Polly Simpson?" Jimmy asked the boy.

"No," answered the boy. "She's Annabel Adams. Her father is the owner of this bank."

Jimmy went to the hotel. He told the hotel clerk that his name was Ralph D. Spencer, and that he had come to Elmore to look for a place (1) he could set up a shoe shop. The clerk was so impressed by Jimmy's clothes and manner that (2)he kindly gave him (about / as / as / he could / much information / the town). Yes, Elmore needed a good shoe shop. It was a pleasant town to live in, and the people were friendly.

"Mr. Spencer" told the hotel clerk that he would like to stay in the town for a few days and look over the situation. Mr. Ralph D. Spencer, Jimmy Valentine's new identity —— an identity created by a sudden attack of love —— remained in Elmore and opened a shoe shop.

Soon his shoe shop was doing a good business, and he won the respect of the community. And more importantly, he got to know Annabel Adams. They fell deeply in (3) and started to plan their wedding.

1. 空所(1)に入る最も適当な語を選びなさい。【文法の知識】　　　　　　　　　　(3点)

　　ア. that　　　　　　イ. what　　　　　ウ. where　　　　エ. which

2. 下線部(2)が「彼は親切にもこの町についてできる限りの情報をジミーに教えた」という意味になるように，(　　)内の語句を適切に並べかえなさい。【表現と文法の知識】　　(4点)

------

3. 空所(3)に入る最も適当な語を答えなさい。【表現の知識・内容についての思考力・判断力・表現力】 (3点)

　　(　　　　　　　　)

4. 次の問いに英語で答えなさい。【内容についての思考力・判断力・表現力】　　　　　　(各5点)

　　(1) How did the hotel clerk feel about Jimmy?

------

　　(2) According to the hotel clerk, what was Elmore like?

A Retrieved Reformation

Part 3

/50

A Translate the English into Japanese and the Japanese into English.【語彙の知識】(各1点)

1. _____ 名 A1　道具，工具　　　2. _____ 副 B1　ひそかに，人知れず

3. _____ 名 A2　ドラッグストア　　4. banker 名 B2　[　　　　　　]

5. softly 副 A2　[　　　　　]　　6. suit 名 A2　[　　　　　　]

B Choose the word whose underlined part is pronounced differently from the other three.【発音の知識】
(各2点)

1. ア. sh<u>oe</u>　　　イ. s<u>ui</u>t　　　ウ. t<u>oo</u>l　　　エ. t<u>ou</u>ch

2. ア. br<u>ea</u>kfast　イ. m<u>e</u>mber　ウ. s<u>e</u>cretly　エ. w<u>e</u>dding

3. ア. arr<u>i</u>ve　　イ. b<u>u</u>siness　ウ. h<u>i</u>mself　エ. unt<u>i</u>l

C Complete the following English sentences to match the Japanese.【表現と文法の知識】
(各3点)

1. この型の携帯電話はもう生産されていません。

This model of cellphone is not produced (　　　　　　).

2. あなたは宿題を提出することを忘れましたよね。

You forgot to submit your homework, (　　　　　　) (　　　　　　)?

3. 彼女は自転車を妹に譲り渡しました。

She (　　　　　) her bicycle (　　　　　　) to her younger sister.

D Arrange the words in the proper order to match the Japanese.【表現と文法の知識・技能】
(各3点)

1. 祖父は1年前にタバコを吸うのをやめました。

My grandfather (a year / ago / finished / smoking / with).

_____

2. 高校のときに私が熱心に取り組んだのは部活動でした。

It (club activities / I / that / was / worked) hard on when I was in high school.

_____

3. 彼は図書館に行く途中にコンビニに寄った。

He stopped at the convenience store (on / the / the library / to / way).

_____

E Read the following passage and answer the questions below.

One day, Jimmy wrote a letter to one of his old friends in Little Rock. The letter said, "I want to give you my tools. You couldn't buy them even for a thousand dollars. (1)(anymore / don't / I / need / them) because I finished with (2)the old business a year ago. I will never touch another man's money again."

It was a few days after Jimmy sent his letter that Ben Price secretly arrived in Elmore. He went around the town in his quiet way until he found out all he wanted to know. From a drugstore across the street from Spencer's shoe shop, he watched Ralph D. Spencer walk (3). "You think you're going to marry the banker's daughter, don't you, Jimmy?" said Ben to himself, softly. "Well, I'm not so sure about that!"

The next morning, Jimmy had breakfast at the Adams home. That day, he was going to Little Rock to order his wedding suit, buy something nice for Annabel, and give his tools away to his friend.

After breakfast, several members of the Adams family went to the bank together —— Mr. Adams, Annabel, Jimmy, and Annabel's married sister with her two little girls, (4) five and nine. On the way to the bank, they waited outside Jimmy's shop while he ran up to his room and got his suitcase. Then they went on to the bank.

1. 下線部(1)の(　　　)内の語を適切に並べかえなさい。【表現と文法の知識】　　　　　(3点)

....

2. 下線部(2)が指す内容として最も適当なものを選びなさい。【内容についての思考力・判断力・表現力】(3点)

　　ア. 銀行員　　　　　　イ. 靴屋　　　　　　　ウ. 金庫破り　　　　　エ. 探偵

3. 空所(3), (4)に入る最も適当な語(句)を選びなさい。【表現と文法の知識】　　　　　(各3点)

　　(3) ア. at　　　　　イ. by　　　　　　ウ. on　　　　　　エ. over
　　(4) ア. age　　　　　イ. aged　　　　　ウ. aging　　　　　エ. having aged

4. 次の問いに英語で答えなさい。【内容についての思考力・判断力・表現力】　　　　　(各4点)

　　(1) Why was Ben going around the town in his quiet way?

....

　　(2) What did Jimmy do while the Adams family was waiting outside his shop?

....

A Retrieved Reformation

Part 4

/50

A Translate the English into Japanese and the Japanese into English.【語彙の知識】(各1点)

1. son-in-law 名 B2   [   ]   2. _____ 動 B1 …を制御する

3. firmly 副 B1   [   ]   4. darkness 名 B1   [   ]

5. _____ 名 A2 恐怖，不安   6. desperate 形 B1   [   ]

B Choose the word whose underlined part is pronounced differently from the other three.【発音の知識】 (各2点)

1. ア. d<u>ar</u>kness   イ. f<u>ir</u>mly   ウ. h<u>ar</u>d   エ. st<u>ar</u>t

2. ア. ch<u>i</u>ldren   イ. <u>i</u>nside   ウ. <u>i</u>nteresting   エ. scr<u>ea</u>m

3. ア. <u>a</u>nything   イ. br<u>ea</u>k   ウ. d<u>e</u>sperate   エ. sp<u>e</u>cial

C Complete the following English sentences to match the Japanese.【表現の知識】 (各3点)

1. 私の母は兄が弁護士であることを誇りに思っています。

My mother (   ) (   ) (   ) her brother being a lawyer.

2. 私は誤って知らない人に電話をかけてしまった。

I called a stranger (   ) (   ).

3. 少しの間待っていただければ，スミス氏に会うことができます。

If you wait (   ) (   ) (   ), you can meet Mr. Smith.

D Arrange the words in the proper order to match the Japanese.【表現と文法の知識・技能】

(各3点)

1. 私たちがテニスの大会で優勝した日のことを覚えていますか。

Do you (we / the day / when / remember / won) the tennis tournament?

2. あなたが昨日カフェで話をしていた男の人はだれですか。

Who (is / talking / the man / were / with / you) at the café yesterday?

3. エマは，そのときすてきなドレスを着ていたのですが，玄関に現れました。

Emma, then (a / dress / nice / wearing), appeared at the front.

E Read the following passage and answer the questions below.

They all went into the banking-room —— Jimmy, too, for Mr. Adams' future son-in-law was welcome anywhere. Everyone in the bank was glad to see the good-looking, nice young man who was going to marry Annabel. Jimmy put down the suitcase in the corner of the room.

The Elmore Bank had just put in a new safe. It was as large as a small room and it had a very special new kind of door that was controlled by a clock. Mr. Adams was very proud of this new safe and was showing how to set the time when the door should open. The two children, May and Agatha, enjoyed (1)(touch) all the interesting parts of its shining heavy door.

While these things were happening, Ben Price quietly entered the bank and looked inside the banking-room. He told the bank teller that he didn't want anything; he was just waiting for a man he knew.

Suddenly, there were screams from the women. May, the five-year-old girl, had firmly closed the door of the safe by accident, and Agatha was inside! Mr. Adams tried hard to pull open the door for a moment, and then cried, "The door can't be opened! And the clock —— I haven't started it yet."

"(2)(it / open / break / please)!" Agatha's mother cried out.

"Quiet!" said Mr. Adams, (3)(raise) a shaking hand. "Everyone, be quiet for a moment. Agatha!" he called as loudly as he could. "Can you hear me?" They could hear, although (4) clearly, the sound of the child's voice. In the darkness inside the safe, she was screaming with fear. Agatha's mother, now getting more desperate, started hitting the door with her hands.

1. 下線部(1), (3)の語を適切な形に変えなさい。【文法の知識】　　　　　　　　(各3点)

(1) _____　　(3) _____

2. 下線部(2)の(　　)内の語を適切に並べかえなさい。【表現と文法の知識】　　(3点)

_____

3. 空所(4)に入る最も適当な語を選びなさい。【文法の知識, 内容についての思考力・判断力・表現力】 (3点)

ア. more　　　　　イ. no　　　　　ウ. not　　　　　エ. very

4. 次の問いに英語で答えなさい。【内容についての思考力・判断力・表現力】　　(各4点)

(1) How large was the new safe?

_____

(2) Who was left inside the safe?

_____

A Retrieved Reformation

Part 5

/50

A Translate the English into Japanese and the Japanese into English.【語彙の知識】(各1点)

1. .... 名 B1 悲嘆，心痛　　　　2. despairing 形　　　[　　　　　　　]

3. .... 副 A2 順調に，円滑に　　4. exhausted 形 B1　[　　　　　　　]

5. unharmed 形　　　[　　　　　　　]　　6. .... 動 B1 ためらう

B Choose the word which has primary stress on a different syllable from the other three.【アクセントの知識】

(各2点)

1. ア. smooth-ly　　イ. min-ute　　ウ. de-spair　　エ. some-thing

2. ア. dis-ap-pear　イ. rec-og-nize　ウ. hes-i-tate　エ. si-lent-ly

3. ア. at-ten-tion　イ. com-plete-ly　ウ. mis-tak-en　エ. un-der-stand

C Complete the following English sentences to match the Japanese.【表現の知識】(各3点)

1. 議長が欠席したので，私が彼の代わりをしました。

Since the chairperson was absent, I (　　　　　　) his (　　　　　　).

2. 朝からずっと，彼は自分の部屋に閉じこもって，宿題をやっていました。

(　　　　　　) the morning (　　　　　　), he stayed in his room and did his homework.

3. 私たちはついに山頂に到着した。

We reached the top of the mountain (　　　　　　) (　　　　　　).

D Arrange the words in the proper order to match the Japanese.【表現と文法の知識・技能】

(各3点)

1. 実験中，私たちは実験室から離れているように言われた。

During the experiment, we were told (away / from / stay / the lab / to).

2. 山道を運転していたとき，大きな石が行く手に立ちはだかった。

When I was driving on a mountain road, (a big stone / in / my / stood / way).

3. 私の言ったことが彼女のプライドを傷つけてしまったかもしれないと心配した。

I (afraid / I / said / that / was / what) might have hurt her pride.

E Read the following passage and answer the questions below.

Annabel turned to Jimmy. Her large eyes were full of pain, but not yet despairing. A woman believes that the man she loves can find a way to do anything. "Can't you do something, Ralph? Try, won't you?" He looked at her with a strange, soft smile on his lips and in his eyes.

"Annabel," he said, "give me that rose you are wearing, will you?"

She couldn't understand what he meant, but she put the rose in his hand. Jimmy took it and placed it in the pocket of his vest. Then he threw off his coat. With that act, Ralph D. Spencer disappeared, and (1)Jimmy Valentine took his place. "Stay away from the door, all of you," he ordered.

He placed his suitcase on the table and opened it. From that time on, he didn't (2)(any / anyone / attention / else / pay / to) there. Quickly he laid the strange shining tools on the table. Nobody moved as they watched him work. Soon Jimmy's drill was biting smoothly into the steel door. In ten minutes —— faster than he had ever done it before —— he opened the door.

Agatha, completely exhausted but unharmed, ran into her mother's arms. Jimmy Valentine silently put his coat back on and walked toward the front door of the bank. As he went, he thought he heard a voice call, "Ralph!" But he never hesitated. At the door, a big man was standing in his way. "Hello, Ben!" said Jimmy. "You're here at last, (3) you? Well, let's go. I don't care now."

"I'm afraid you're mistaken, Mr. Spencer," said Ben Price. "I don't believe I recognize you." Then the big detective turned away and walked slowly down the street.

1. 下線部(1)が指す内容として最も適当なものを選びなさい。【内容についての思考力・判断力・表現力】(3点)

　　ア. 銀行員になる　　　イ. 金庫破りになる　　ウ. 探偵になる　　　　エ. 新郎になる

2. 下線部(2)の(　　)内の語を適切に並べかえなさい。【表現と文法の知識】　　　　　　　(4点)

3. 空所(3)に入る最も適当な語を選びなさい。【表現と文法の知識】　　　　　　　　　　(3点)

　　ア. are　　　　　　　イ. aren't　　　　　ウ. do　　　　　　　エ. don't

4. 次の問いに英語で答えなさい。【内容についての思考力・判断力・表現力】　　　　　(各5点)

　　(1) How long did it take Jimmy to break the safe open?

　　(2) Did Ben arrest Jimmy?

Ask Friends and Followers for Advice on Social Media

/50

A Translate the English into Japanese and the Japanese into English.【語彙の知識】(各1点)

1. ＿＿＿＿＿＿＿＿ 名 A2　助言
2. ＿＿＿＿＿＿＿＿ 名 B2　支持者, フォロワー
3. brass band 名　[　　　　]
4. ＿＿＿＿＿＿＿＿ 形 B2　(時間が)空いた
5. wisely 副　[　　　　]
6. ＿＿＿＿＿＿＿＿ 形　すがすがしい

B Choose the word whose underlined part is pronounced differently from the other three.【発音の知識】(各2点)

1. ア. adv<u>i</u>ce　　イ. g<u>i</u>ve　　ウ. m<u>i</u>nd　　エ. w<u>i</u>sely
2. ア. f<u>o</u>llower　　イ. <u>o</u>ther　　ウ. pr<u>o</u>blem　　エ. sh<u>o</u>p
3. ア. <u>air</u>　　イ. <u>ear</u>ly　　ウ. sh<u>are</u>　　エ. sp<u>are</u>

C Complete the following English sentences to match the Japanese.【表現と文法の知識】

(各3点)

1. 私はよく母にアドバイスを求めます。

   I often (　　　　　　) my mother (　　　　　　) advice.

2. 雨の日はバスに乗らなければならない。

   On a rainy day, I have to (　　　　　　) (　　　　　　) a bus.

3. この道路を渡るときは注意したほうがいいよ。

   (　　　　　) (　　　　　) (　　　　　) careful when you cross this road.

D Arrange the words in the proper order to match the Japanese.【表現と文法の知識・技能】

(各3点)

1. 私が出張に出ている間に犬の世話をしてもらえませんか。

   Will you take care of my dog (am / away / business / I / on / while)?

   ＿＿＿＿＿＿＿＿＿＿＿＿＿＿＿＿＿＿＿＿＿＿＿＿＿＿＿＿＿＿＿＿

2. しばらく休憩したらどうですか。

   (a rest / don't / take / why / you) for a while?

   ＿＿＿＿＿＿＿＿＿＿＿＿＿＿＿＿＿＿＿＿＿＿＿＿＿＿＿＿＿＿＿＿

3. 決断する時間を少しあげます。

   I will (decide / give / some / time / to / you).

   ＿＿＿＿＿＿＿＿＿＿＿＿＿＿＿＿＿＿＿＿＿＿＿＿＿＿＿＿＿＿＿＿

E Read the following passage and answer the questions below.

Nyanko

Our brass band practice is very hard every day. After practice, I ride on the train for about one hour and get home late. After I eat dinner and take a bath, it is already 9:30 p.m. I'm always (1)! How can I study? Please give me some good advice.

Yujin: (2) your spare time wisely. (3), you can study while you are on the train.

Ribrib: Why don't you get up early and study in the early morning? I do (4)it. It's really refreshing.

David: You should (5)(about / and other / band members / tell / your teacher) your problem. They may give you good advice.

1. 空所(1)〜(3)に入る最も適当な語句を選びなさい。【語彙と文法の知識】　　　（各2点）

    (1) ア. tired and sleep　　　　　　イ. tired and sleepy
       ウ. tiring and sleep　　　　　　エ. tiring and sleepy
    (2) ア. Use　　　　イ. Used　　　　ウ. Using　　　　エ. To use
    (3) ア. As a result　　　　　　イ. However
       ウ. On the other hand　　　　エ. For example

2. 下線部(4)は具体的には何を指していますか。日本語で答えなさい。
   　　　　　　　　　　　　　　　　　　【内容についての思考力・判断力・表現力】　（3点）

   ....

3. 下線部(5)の(　　　)内の語句を適切に並べかえなさい。【表現の知識】　　　　（3点）

   ....

4. 次の問いに英語で答えなさい。【内容についての思考力・判断力・表現力】　　　（各4点）

   (1) How long does Nyanko ride on the train to get home from school?

   ....

   (2) According to Ribrib, what is refreshing?

   ....

Let's Buy Fair-trade Chocolate!

/50

A Translate the English into Japanese and the Japanese into English.【語彙の知識】(各1点)

1. .... 形 B1 熱帯の　　　　　2. delicate 形 B1 　　[　　　　　　　]

3. .... 名 A2 貿易　　　　　　4. .... 名 B2 利益, 収益

5. sustainable 形　　[　　　　　　　]　6. fund 名 B1　　[　　　　　　　]

B Choose the word whose underlined part is pronounced differently from the other three.【発音の知識】

(各2点)

1. ア. ar<u>ea</u>　　　　イ. <u>ea</u>sy　　　　ウ. l<u>ea</u>flet　　　　エ. w<u>ea</u>k

2. ア. <u>e</u>nvironment　イ. <u>i</u>llness　　ウ. m<u>o</u>ment　　エ. probl<u>e</u>m

3. ア. <u>ca</u>cao　　　　イ. f<u>a</u>vorite　　ウ. st<u>a</u>tion　　エ. tr<u>a</u>der

C Complete the following English sentences to match the Japanese.【表現と文法の知識】

(各3点)

1. その子たちはドーナツが好きかもしれません。

　The kids (　　　　　　) (　　　　　　　) donuts.

2. そのヒーローは子供たちを暴力から守りました。

　The hero (　　　　　　) the children (　　　　　　) violence.

3. あなたのおかげで時間に間に合いました。

　(　　　　　　) (　　　　　　　) you, I could make it in time.

D Arrange the words in the proper order to match the Japanese.【表現と文法の知識・技能】

(各3点)

1. あなたの英語のスキルはよくなっていますよ。

　(better / English / getting / is / skill / your).

　..

2. 母は私のゲーム機を取り上げました。

　(away / gaming machine / my / my mother / took).

　..

3. ジャックは去年自分で事業を立ち上げました。

　Jack (business / his / own / set / up) last year.

　..

E Read the following passage and answer the questions below.

You Can Make a Difference in Farmers' Lives!

Chocolate may be your favorite food. But (1)do you (cacao trees / growing / hard / is / know / work)? Cacao trees grow in hot, rainy, tropical places. Cacao plants are delicate.

Small family farmers grow about 90% of the world's cacao. They must protect trees (2) wind, sun, insects and illness. Cacao prices are rising, (3) the farmers get very little from its trade. The traders take away much of the profit.

Thanks to fair-trade, cacao farming can be sustainable. We buy cacao beans from those small farmers (4) fair prices. We set up local funds, too. Fair-trade has rules about farming to protect the environment.

Why don't you buy fair-trade chocolate? (5)That can be a great help for cacao farmers.

1. 下線部(1)が「カカオの木を育てるのは大変な仕事であることを知っていますか」という意味になるように，（　）内の語句を適切に並べかえなさい。【表現と文法の知識】　　　(3点)

_____

2. 空所(2)，(4)に入る最も適当な語を選びなさい。【語彙と表現の知識】　　　(各2点)
   (2) ア. for 　　　　イ. from 　　　　ウ. on 　　　　エ. with
   (4) ア. at 　　　　イ. by 　　　　ウ. in 　　　　エ. on

3. 空所(3)に入る最も適当な接続詞を答えなさい。【語彙の知識, 内容についての思考力・判断力・表現力】　(2点)
   (　　　　　　　)

4. 下線部(5)は具体的には何を指していますか。日本語で答えなさい。
   【内容についての思考力・判断力・表現力】　(3点)

_____

5. 次の問いに英語で答えなさい。【内容についての思考力・判断力・表現力】　　　(各4点)
   (1) Who grows most of cacao in the world?

   _____

   (2) Why do cacao farmers get very little from its trade?

   _____

Good to Be Different

/50

A Translate the English into Japanese and the Japanese into English. 【語彙の知識】(各1点)

1. _____ 形 B1 競争の，競争的な　　2. train 動 A2　　[　　　　　]

3. _____ 動 A1 焦点を当てる，集中する　　4. logically 副　　[　　　　　]

5. _____ 動 B1 …に頼る　　6. feeling 名 A1　　[　　　　　]

B Choose the word which has primary stress on a different syllable from the other three. 【アクセントの知識】

(各2点)

1. ア. e-nough　　イ. re-lieve　　ウ. re-ly　　エ. swim-mer

2. ア. Aus-tral-ia　　イ. dif-fer-ence　　ウ. in-ter-view　　エ. qual-i-ty

3. ア. del-i-cate　　イ. ex-am-ple　　ウ. per-form-ance　　エ. re-fresh-ing

C Complete the following English sentences to match the Japanese. 【表現の知識】(各3点)

1. ときには人の助けに頼るといいよ。

You should sometimes (　　　　　) (　　　　　) other people's help.

2. 彼女は私の人生に大きな影響を与えた。

She has had a major (　　　　　) (　　　　　) my life.

3. 多くの人が彼を英雄だとみなしていたが，彼はそのことが嫌だった。

Many people (　　　　) him (　　　　　) a hero, but he did not like it.

D Arrange the words in the proper order to match the Japanese. 【表現と文法の知識・技能】

(各3点)

1. 私は一つの活動に集中するのが苦手だ。

I (am / at / focusing / good / not / on) one activity.

_____

2. だれがそんなことをするように言ったの？

Who (do / that / to / told / you)?

_____

3. あなたの友達でいられてうれしいです。

It (be / friends / is / nice / to / with) you.

_____

E Read the following passage and answer the questions below.

Reporter: (1)(like / the Rio Paralympics / was / what) for you?

Mei: I felt relieved when I was (2)(choose) for the Japanese team. People hoped I could get a medal, but I knew I wasn't good enough.

Reporter: After Rio, you trained in Australia for three months. What did you learn there?

Mei: Before (3)that, I just tried hard to get a good result. (4), Australian swimmers focused on the quality of their swimming. I learned to think logically about my own performance, and not just rely too much on feelings.

Reporter: Who had an impact on your way of (5)(think)?

Mei: My mom and dad. They told me it's good to be different. I hope (6)(an individual / as / each person / people / see).

1. 下線部(1), (6)の(　　)内の語句を適切に並べかえなさい。【表現と文法の知識】　　(各2点)

   (1) _____

   (6) _____

2. 下線部(2), (5)の語を適切な形に変えなさい。【語彙と文法の知識】　　(各2点)

   (2) _____

   (5) _____

3. 下線部(3)は具体的には何を指していますか。日本語で答えなさい。

【内容についての思考力・判断力・表現力】 (2点)

_____

4. 空所(4)に入る最も適当な語句を選びなさい。【表現の知識, 内容についての思考力・判断力・表現力】 (2点)

   ア. For example　　　　　　　イ. For the first time

   ウ. In the same way　　　　　エ. On the other hand

5. 次の問いに英語で答えなさい。【内容についての思考力・判断力・表現力】　　(各4点)

   (1) Where did Mei train for three months after the Rio Paralympics?

   _____

   (2) What did Mei's parents tell her?

   _____

Welcome to an Esports Tournament!

/50

A Translate the English into Japanese and the Japanese into English.【語彙の知識】(各1点)

1. ＿＿＿＿＿ 動 B1　参加する　　　　2. structure 名 A2　　　[　　　　　　]

3. ＿＿＿＿＿ 名 A2　参加費　　　　　4. unofficial 形 B2　　[　　　　　　]

5. register 動 B1　　　[　　　　　]　6. ＿＿＿＿＿ 名 B1　締め切り，期限

B Choose the word whose underlined part is pronounced differently from the other three.【発音の知識】　　　　　　　　　　　　　　　　　　　　(各2点)

1. ア．center　　　イ．circle　　　ウ．participate　　　エ．unofficial

2. ア．shoulder　　イ．soul　　　ウ．timezone　　　エ．welcome

3. ア．danger　　　イ．game　　　ウ．logically　　　エ．registration

C Complete the following English sentences to match the Japanese.【表現の知識】　(各3点)

1. 高校生ならだれでもこのコンテストに参加できます。

Any high school student can (　　　　　　) (　　　　　　) this contest.

2. 日本へようこそ。

(　　　　　　) (　　　　　　) Japan.

3. その腕時計を修理するのに少なくとも 8 ドル必要だ。

You need (　　　　　　) (　　　　　　) 8 dollars to repair the watch.

D Arrange the words in the proper order to match the Japanese.【表現と文法の知識・技能】

(各3点)

1. またあなたといっしょに仕事ができるのを楽しみにしています。

I'm (forward / looking / to / with / working / you) again.

＿＿＿＿＿＿＿＿＿＿＿＿＿＿＿＿＿＿＿＿＿＿＿＿

2. 私たちの状況を理解していただきありがとうございます。

(for / thank / understanding / we / you) our situation.

＿＿＿＿＿＿＿＿＿＿＿＿＿＿＿＿＿＿＿＿＿＿＿＿

3. ホテルから出てはいけません。

(go / must / not / of / out / you) the hotel.

＿＿＿＿＿＿＿＿＿＿＿＿＿＿＿＿＿＿＿＿＿＿＿＿

E Read the following passage and answer the questions below.

Dream Matches Asian HS Tournament
by Sakura Gaming Online – July 20

Welcome to Dream Matches, Asian HS Tournament by Sakura Gaming. This is a tournament for Asian high school students of all skill levels. We are looking forward to (1)(see) the fighting spirit of all players. We thank you for participating (2) this exciting event!

Date & Time: Match 1 | July 20, 2021 | 6 p.m.

Match 2 | July 20, 2021 | 7 p.m.

Structure: 25 Teams | 1 match

Timezone: Tokyo (UTC+9:00)

Fees: Free to play matches

Rules:1. Each team needs at least eight players to participate.

2. All players in the tournament must have ESPORTS accounts.

3. Players (3) use any unofficial versions of games.

4. Players (3) use unofficial items.

5. All team players must register (4) the deadline.

After registration, players will get more information about the event.

Registration is now open and will run until July 20, 2021, 4 p.m. JST.

1. 下線部(1)の語を適切な形に変えなさい。【表現と文法の知識】　　　　　　　　(3点)

....

2. 空所(2), (4)に入る最も適当な語を選びなさい。【語彙と表現の知識】　　　　　(各3点)

(2) ア. at　　　　　　イ. for　　　　　　ウ. in　　　　　　エ. to

(4) ア. at　　　　　　イ. by　　　　　　ウ. from　　　　　エ. on

3. 空所(3)に共通して入る最も適当な語(句)を選びなさい。

【内容についての思考力・判断力・表現力】　(3点)

ア. don't have to　　イ. may not　　　ウ. must not　　　エ. should

4. 次の問いに英語で答えなさい。【内容についての思考力・判断力・表現力】　　　(各4点)

(1) How much does it cost to play in the tournament?

....

(2) When will players get more information about the event?

....

Additional Lesson 5 — "Favorite" Encounters

/50

A Translate the English into Japanese and the Japanese into English. 【語彙の知識】 (各1点)

1. encounter 動 B2   [   ]   2. .... 名 A2   道具, 器具

3. challenging 形 B1   [   ]   4. .... 動 A2 · …を励ます

5. .... 動 B1 …を表現する   6. collaborate 動   [   ]

B Choose the word which has primary stress on a different syllable from the other three. 【アクセントの知識】   (各2点)

1. ア. ex-press   イ. per-form   ウ. re-ly   エ. some-times

2. ア. en-coun-ter   イ. chal-leng-ing   ウ. in-stru-ment   エ. var-i-ous

3. ア. col-lab-o-rate   イ. com-mu-ni-cate   ウ. log-i-cal-ly   エ. pro-fes-sion-al

C Complete the following English sentences to match the Japanese. 【表現の知識】 (各3点)

1. 私は10歳のときにこの街へ引っ越してきた。

I moved to this town at (   ) (   ) (   ) ten.

2. ダンスを通して自分自身を表現できます。

I can (   ) (   ) through dance.

3. 私たちはあなたがたの会社に協力できてうれしいです。

We are glad that we could (   ) (   ) your company.

D Arrange the words in the proper order to match the Japanese. 【表現と文法の知識・技能】

(各3点)

1. 子供たちにとってその山に登るのは大変だった。

It (challenging / climb / for / the children / to / was) the mountain.

2. 私は息子が一生懸命に練習していたことに感銘を受けた。

I (impressed / my son / practicing / was / with) hard.

3. 彼のアドバイスに励まされて, 私は勉強をさらに頑張れた。

His advice (encouraged / harder / me / study / to).

E Read the following passage and answer the questions below.

I was born (1) an American father and a Japanese mother. I went to Yokohama International School. Sometimes (2)it was challenging for me to communicate in English at school. I first encountered the *koto* at the age of nine. I loved playing the musical instrument during my first Japanese music classes because I could make beautiful sounds (3) it easily.

I was first taught by Mr. Patterson. He has lived in Japan since 1986 and performs and teaches the *koto*. He is a great teacher.

My classmates were impressed with my playing and this encouraged me to work harder. I (4)(easier / express / it / realized / that / to / was) myself through the *koto* than with words.

I became a professional *koto* player in 2017, and now I enjoy (5)(collaborate) with various artists.

1. 空所(1), (3)に入る最も適当な語を選びなさい。【語彙と表現の知識】　　　　　(各2点)

   (1) ア. from　　　　イ. in　　　　　ウ. on　　　　　エ. to

   (3) ア. as　　　　　イ. for　　　　　ウ. in　　　　　エ. with

2. 下線部(2)は具体的には何を指していますか。日本語で答えなさい。【文法の知識】　　(3点)

      ....

3. 下線部(4)の(　　)内の語を適切に並べかえなさい。【表現と文法の知識】　　　(3点)

      ....

4. 下線部(5)の語を適切な形に変えなさい。【文法の知識】　　　　　　　　　　(2点)

      ....

5. 次の問いに英語で答えなさい。【内容についての思考力・判断力・表現力】　　　(各4点)

   (1) When did Leo encounter the *koto*?

      ....

   (2) Why was Leo encouraged to work harder?

      ....

Additional Lesson 6 — Japanese Students Appeal for World Peace

/50

A Translate the English into Japanese and the Japanese into English.【語彙の知識】(各1点)

1. ＿＿＿＿＿＿＿＿ 形 A2　平和な，安らかな　　2. conference 名 B2　　[　　　　　　]

3. submit 動 B2　　[　　　　　　]　　4. abolition 名 B1　　[　　　　　　]

5. ＿＿＿＿＿＿＿＿ 形 B1　核の　　　　　　6. ＿＿＿＿＿＿＿＿ 名　武器，兵器

B Choose the word whose underlined part is pronounced differently from the other three.【発音の知識】

(各2点)

1. ア. <u>a</u>mbassador　　イ. <u>a</u>ttend　　ウ. ch<u>a</u>llenge　　エ. ch<u>a</u>rity

2. ア. ab<u>o</u>lition　　イ. ch<u>i</u>ldren　　ウ. real<u>i</u>ze　　エ. s<u>i</u>gnature

3. ア. includ<u>i</u>ng　　イ. r<u>u</u>le　　ウ. sch<u>oo</u>l　　エ. s<u>u</u>bmit

C Complete the following English sentences to match the Japanese.【表現と文法の知識】

(各3点)

1. 生徒会長は毎年9月に選ばれます。

The president of student council (　　　　　) (　　　　　) every September.

2. 英語の先生は，私たちの考えに賛同して，たくさん助けてくれました。

Our English teacher helped us a lot in (　　　　　) of our idea.

3. 外はとても寒い。加えて，雪も降っている。

It's so cold outside. (　　　　　) (　　　　　), it's snowing.

D Arrange the words in the proper order to match the Japanese.【表現と文法の知識・技能】

(各3点)

1. 私たちは，このアスリートがマイナーなスポーツを人気スポーツに変える力があると信じている。

We believe this athlete (change / has / into / minor sports / the power / to) popular sports.

＿＿＿＿＿＿＿＿＿＿＿＿＿＿＿＿＿＿＿＿＿＿＿＿＿＿＿＿＿＿＿＿＿＿

2. 太郎は卒業式ですばらしいスピーチをした。

Taro (a / at / great / made / speech / the graduation ceremony).

＿＿＿＿＿＿＿＿＿＿＿＿＿＿＿＿＿＿＿＿＿＿＿＿＿＿＿＿＿＿＿＿＿＿

3. 私たちは貧しい子供たちのために寄付を呼びかけた。

We (appealed / donations / for / for / poor children).

＿＿＿＿＿＿＿＿＿＿＿＿＿＿＿＿＿＿＿＿＿＿＿＿＿＿＿＿＿＿＿＿＿＿

E Read the following passage and answer the questions below.

Japanese High School Students Go to the U.N.

Do you think young people have the power to change the world? Now, the world knows that some Japanese high school students have worked hard to help to create a peaceful world.

Japanese High School Student Peace Ambassadors are chosen every year from around the country. (1)They attend many conferences, including one at the United Nations Office. There, they make speeches in English to appeal for world peace. They also submit signatures they (2)(collected / have / in / of / support / the abolition) of nuclear weapons.

(3), the ambassadors do some charity activities. They collect pencils and other stationery, and they send them to some poor countries. They also (4)(_____) a charity fund for poor children in Asia.

In total, more than 200 students have worked hard for peace since 1998. Their voices have reached many people around the world.

1. 下線部(1)を日本語に訳しなさい。【表現と文法の知識】 (3点)

_____

2. 下線部(2)の(   )内の語句を適切に並べかえなさい。【表現と文法の知識】 (3点)

_____

3. 空所(3)に入る最も適当な語句を選びなさい。【表現の知識】 (3点)

    ア. First of all   イ. For example   ウ. In addition   エ. In contrast

4. 下線部(4)が「慈善基金を運営する」という意味になるように，(   )に適語を補いなさい。

    (   )　　　　　　　　　　　　　　　　　　　　　　【語彙と表現の知識】 (3点)

5. 次の問いに英語で答えなさい。【内容についての思考力・判断力・表現力】 (各4点)

    (1) What do the ambassadors collect in order to send to some poor countries?

    _____

    (2) How many students have worked for peace so far?

    _____

The Changing Meaning of "Convenience"

/50

A Translate the English into Japanese and the Japanese into English. 【語彙の知識】（各1点）

1. chart 名 A2   [   ]   2. _____ 動 B1 …に順応する

3. constantly 副 B1   [   ]   4. _____ 動 A2 …と取り替える

5. _____ 形 A2 年配の，年老いた   6. delivery 名 B1   [   ]

B Choose the word which has primary stress on a different syllable from the other three. 【アクセントの知識】   （各2点）

1. ア. a-dapt   イ. de-mand   ウ. prod-uct   エ. re-place

2. ア. at-ten-tion   イ. con-stant-ly   ウ. cus-tom-er   エ. eld-er-ly

3. ア. am-bas-sa-dor   イ. de-liv-er-y   ウ. dis-ad-van-tage   エ. so-ci-e-ty

C Complete the following English sentences to match the Japanese. 【表現と文法の知識】

（各3点）

1. 以前は公園の中に大きな木があった。

   There (   ) (   ) (   ) a big tree in the park.

2. 近年この学校の生徒数は減少している。

   In recent years, the number of students in this school (   )
(   ) (   ).

3. 彼は彼女が嘘をついていると言ったが，私はそんなことはないと確信している。

   He said that she told a lie, but I am sure that it is (   )
(   ) (   ).

D Arrange the words in the proper order to match the Japanese. 【表現と文法の知識・技能】

（各3点）

1. 私たちの会社は5年前とはまったく違っている。

   Our company is (different / from / it / quite / was / what) five years ago.

2. この町の食料品の値段は，私の故郷よりも2倍近く高い。

   The price of food in this city is (as / as / high / nearly / that / twice) in my
hometown.

3. 将来，ますます多くの人が一人でキャンプに行くだろう。

   (and / camping / go / more / more / people / will) alone in the future.

E Read the following passage and answer the questions below.

The number of convenience stores in Japan has been growing. Convenience stores (1)(are / drop / easy / into / to). Their products are constantly changing. Every year, about 70% of all products are replaced by new ones. This is because of demand from society.

The customers of convenience stores used to be mainly young people, but these days, (2)that is not the case. According (3) the graph, in 2017, the number of customers aged 50 or over (4)(as / as / four / times / large / was) that in 1989.

There will be more and more elderly people in the future. Home delivery of products will become more common for people who cannot travel easily. They can order what they need online and get it at home. (5) our society is changing, the meaning of "convenience" can also change.

1. 下線部(1), (4)の(　　)内の語を適切に並べかえなさい。【表現と文法の知識】　　　　　(各3点)

　　(1) ....

　　(4) ....

2. 下線部(2)は具体的には何を指していますか。日本語で答えなさい。

　　　　　　　　　　　　　　　　　　　　　　　　【内容についての思考力・判断力・表現力】　(2点)

　　...

3. 空所(3)に入る最も適当な前置詞を答えなさい。【表現の知識】　　　　　　　　　　　(2点)

　　(　　　　　　　　　)

4. 空所(5)に入る最も適当な語を選びなさい。【語彙の知識】　　　　　　　　　　　　(2点)

　　ア. As　　　　　　　イ. In　　　　　　　ウ. With　　　　　エ. Without

5. 次の問いに英語で答えなさい。【内容についての思考力・判断力・表現力】　　　　　(各4点)

　　(1) What percentage of convenience stores' products are replaced by new ones every year?

　　...

　　(2) What is home delivery like?

　　...

Machine Translation: No Need to Learn English?

/50

A Translate the English into Japanese and the Japanese into English.【語彙の知識】(各1点)

1. _____ 名 B2 翻訳

2. statistically 副 [   ]

3. appropriate 形 A2 [   ]

4. _____ 名 B2 データ, 情報

5. _____ 動 B1 …を翻訳する

6. inaccurate 形 B2 [   ]

B Choose the word whose underlined part is pronounced differently from the other three.【発音の知識】(各2点)

1. ア. ch<u>e</u>ck　　イ. <u>ch</u>icken　　ウ. <u>ch</u>ild　　エ. ma<u>ch</u>ine

2. ア. d<u>a</u>ta　　イ. ex<u>a</u>mple　　ウ. repl<u>a</u>ce　　エ. transl<u>a</u>te

3. ア. act<u>i</u>vity　　イ. ret<u>u</u>rn　　ウ. stat<u>i</u>stically　　エ. unn<u>a</u>tural

C Complete the following English sentences to match the Japanese.【表現の知識】(各3点)

1. その女の子は大きなチョコレートを小さく分けた。

The girl (   ) (   ) the big chocolate (   ) small pieces.

2. あなたの名前をこの機械に入力してください。

Please (   ) your name (   ) this machine.

3. あなたが簡単に理解できるように例を挙げてみましょう。

I'll (   ) an (   ) for you to understand easily.

D Arrange the words in the proper order to match the Japanese.【表現と文法の知識・技能】

(各3点)

1. 彼の弱みがわからない。

(can't / find / his / I / out / weakness).

_____

2. ジムがどうやってここへ来たか知っていますか。

(came / do / how / Jim / know / you) here?

_____

3. 自分自身を信じ続けることが大切です。

(believing / important / is / it / keep / to) in yourself.

_____

E Read the following passage and answer the questions below.

Machine translation is simple. The machine statistically finds out the most appropriate match from translation data. A set of data is like: "髪が長くなった; My hair got longer." It is broken up into smaller pieces, (1) "髪; my hair" and "長くなった; got longer." When you put "日が長くなった" (2) machine translation, the machine matches the best pieces of data and produces "The day (3)."

However, machine translation has (4)<u>several problems</u>. If translated sentences are inaccurate, we must correct them. In addition, it is sometimes difficult for us to recognize inaccurate translations.

If we take an example, like "部活で帰りが遅くなった," we can see how inaccurate sometimes machine translation is.

部活で帰りが遅くなった。⇒ My return got late in club activities.

This machine translation is very unnatural. You should say, "I returned home late because of my club activities." So it is still important for us to keep learning English hard.

1. 空所(1), (2)に入る最も適当な語(句)を選びなさい。【表現の知識】 （各2点）

  (1) ア. in addition   イ. in fact   ウ. in short   エ. such as

  (2) ア. into   イ. on   ウ. through   エ. with

2. 空所(3)に入る最も適当な表現を，文脈から判断して答えなさい。

【内容についての思考力・判断力・表現力】 （3点）

----

3. 下線部(4)のseveral problemsとは具体的にはどのような問題か。日本語で2点答えなさい。

【内容についての思考力・判断力・表現力】 （完答5点）

----

4. 次の問いに英語で答えなさい。【内容についての思考力・判断力・表現力】 （各4点）

  (1) What is a correct English translation of "部活で帰りが遅くなった"?

----

  (2) Do we still need to learn English hard?

A Boy Helps to Solve the Microplastic Problem

/50

A Translate the English into Japanese and the Japanese into English.【語彙の知識】(各1点)

1. discovery 名 B1　　[　　　　　]　　2. ＿＿＿＿＿＿＿ 形 B2　世界的な

3. finally 副 A2　　[　　　　　]　　4. disappear 動 A2　　[　　　　　　]

5. ＿＿＿＿＿＿＿ 名 B1　実験　　　　6. billion 名 B2　　[　　　　　　]

B Choose the word which has primary stress on a different syllable from the other three.【アクセントの知識】(各2点)

1. ア. plas-tic　　　イ. mi-crobe　　　ウ. bil-lion　　　エ. a-gain

2. ア. In-ter-net　　イ. fi-nal-ly　　　ウ. dis-ap-pear　　エ. pow-er-ful

3. ア. in-for-ma-tion　イ. Ca-na-di-an　ウ. dis-cov-er-y　エ. ex-per-i-ment

C Complete the following English sentences to match the Japanese.【表現・文法の知識】(各3点)

1. 彼はそのレポートを終わらせるのに1週間かかった。

　It (　　　　　) him a week (　　　　　) (　　　　　) the report.

2. 世界で何十億もの人がその映画を見ました。

　(　　　　　) (　　　　　) people around the world have seen the movie.

3. 彼女は厳しい練習に耐えた。その結果，レギュラーに選ばれた。

　She endured hard training. (　　　　　) (　　　　　) (　　　　　), she was selected as a regular player.

D Arrange the words in the proper order to match the Japanese.【表現と文法の知識・技能】(各3点)

1. 私はその手紙を何度も読みました。

　I (again / again / and / read / the letter).

＿＿＿＿＿＿＿＿＿＿＿＿＿＿＿＿＿＿＿＿＿＿＿＿＿＿＿

2. 母は私に散らかっていた部屋を片付けさせました。

　(clean / made / me / my mother / up) my messy room.

＿＿＿＿＿＿＿＿＿＿＿＿＿＿＿＿＿＿＿＿＿＿＿＿＿＿＿

3. トムは私のスーツケースを2階まで運ぶのを手伝ってくれた。

　Tom (carry / helped / me / my suitcase / upstairs).

＿＿＿＿＿＿＿＿＿＿＿＿＿＿＿＿＿＿＿＿＿＿＿＿＿＿＿

E Read the following passage and answer the questions below.

A Boy's Discovery May Solve the Microplastic Problem

Microplastic pollution is a worldwide problem today. A Canadian boy has given us a good answer to it. Daniel Burd, a 16-year-old high school student, showed his research on microbes that could eat plastics. He (1)(win) the top prize at the Canada-Wide Science Fair.

Daniel said, "Plastics finally break down and disappear, (2) it usually takes 1,000 years to do so. This means some microbes can eat plastics slowly." Then he asked himself, "Can I make those microbes do (3)the job faster?" He did his experiment (4). At last, he found the most powerful type of microbe.

About 500 billion plastic bags are used worldwide each year. Billions of (5)these end up in the oceans. Animals eat those plastic bags, and as a result, the animals often die. Daniel's discovery will help us solve the microplastic problem.

1. 下線部(1)の語を適切な形に変えなさい。【文法の知識】　　　　　　　　　　　　　(2点)

　　..

2. 空所(2), (4)に入る最も適当な語(句)を選びなさい。【語彙と表現の知識】　　　　(各2点)

　　(2) ア. as　　　　　　イ. because　　　　ウ. since　　　　　エ. though
　　(4) ア. again and again　　　　　イ. for the first time
　　　　ウ. once　　　　　　　　　エ. twice

3. 下線部(3), (5)が指すものとして最も適当なものを選びなさい。

　　　　　　　　　　　　　　　　　　　　【内容についての思考力・判断力・表現力】　(各3点)

　　(3) ア. doing experiment　　　　イ. doing research
　　　　ウ. eating plastics　　　　　エ. growing up
　　(5) ア. animals　　イ. garbage　　ウ. microbes　　エ. plastic bags

4. 次の問いに英語で答えなさい。【内容についての思考力・判断力・表現力】　　　　(各4点)

　　(1) What has Daniel given us?

　　..

　　(2) What did Daniel finally find?

　　..